You *Can* Take It with You

YOU CAN TAKE IT

THE EXCITEMENT OF
PERSONAL WITNESSING
FOR CHRIST

WITH YOU

BO MITCHELL
Foreword by Larry Lewis

BROADMAN PRESS
Nashville, Tennessee

ISBN: 0-8054-5739-9
Dewey Decimal Classification: 248.5
Subject Heading: WITNESSING
Library of Congress Catalog Number: 89-33093

Printed in the United States of America

Unless otherwise stated, all Scripture quotations are from the King James Version of the Bible.

Scripture quotations marked NIV are from HOLY BIBLE: *New International Version,* copyright © 1973, 1978, 1984 by International Bible Society.

Scripture quotations marked Williams are from the *Williams New Testament, the New Testament in the Language of the People,* by Charles B. Williams. Copyright © 1937, 1966, 1986 by Holman Bible Publishers. Used by permission.

Library of Congress Cataloging-in-Publication Data

Mitchell, Bo, 1923-
    You can take it with you / Bo Mitchell ; foreword by Larry Lewis ;
introduction by Howard Ramsey.
        p.   cm.
    ISBN 0-8054-5739-9 :
    1. Witness bearing (Christianity)   2. Evangelistic work.
3. Mitchell, Bo, 1923-   I. Title.
BV4520.M556   1990
248'.5—dc20
                                                                89-33093
                                                                CIP

To Mickie, my dearest, and our three sons
Gary, Ron, and Brad;
to our daughters Marcie and Jean and our
grandsons Blake, Justin, Benjie, and
Matthew.
How God does manifest His unbounded love
through the miraculous gift of family!

Contents

Foreword

Jesus' last words called His disciples to their first priority, *being witnesses for Him.*

Much of the Christian church finds itself impotent and powerless in today's world. It hesitates, debates, and for the most part declines. Yet, the lost world rushes on toward eternal damnation. Philosophy, wealth, education, pleasure, and scores of cults and religions all miss the mark. The devil's snares abound!

In His last words to His disciples, Jesus commanded, *"You will be my witnesses* in Jerusalem, Judea and Samaria and to the ends of the earth." Acts 1:8 (NIV) Our Lord's early followers accepted His command and challenge and the known world was revolutionized! It could happen again today. Lost souls by the millions wait for someone with the answer. Christians have the only answer—Jesus Christ Himself!

You Can Take It with You will bring tears to your eyes and conviction to your soul. This excellent book by one of America's outstanding soul-winners will be mightily used of God to make more fervent, faithful witnesses of those who read its pages.

Jesus' last words called His disciples to their first priority, being witnesses for Him. *You Can Take It with You* can be your guide.

Larry Lewis, president
Home Mission Board, SBC
Atlanta, Georgia

Introduction

by Howard Ramsey

I first met the author, Bo Mitchell, in July 1979, at an evangelism equipping task force meeting. Before we were introduced, I observed him sharing the Gospel with a lost hotel employee. The next time we met, in January 1980, before we finished eating lunch, he shared his testimony and a gospel booklet with a waitress. It was then the Lord directed me to invite him and his wife, Mickie, to serve as Mission Service Corps volunteers with the Personal Evangelism Department of the Home Mission Board. For over eight years I have continued to observe that he believes and practices his motto, "Words of witness can be given in the church house, school classes, in a neighborhood yard, in houses, at work, and in the street by men, women, youth, children and preachers anywhere and everywhere as God opens the door."

Every pastor, staff member, layperson and denominational worker will benefit from reading this book. It may well be the impetus that ignites the movement which began in the early seventies of equipping and involving all Christians in the task of soul-winning.

Bo Mitchell is a product of the movement and is being used of God to challenge and motivate pastors and laypersons to take seriously the command of our Lord, "But you will receive power when the Holy Spirit comes on you, and you will be my witnesses in Jerusalem, and in all Judea and Samaria, and to the ends of the earth." (Acts 1:8, NIV).

Those who read the book will be encouraged and rebuked as they identify with the pilgrimage of Bo Mitchell. Wives who are praying for husbands will rejoice when they learn that his wife, Mickie, her Sunday School teachers and class members had prayed for several years before, on his 33rd birthday, Bo suddenly decided to attend church. Pastors who desire to see people saved but do not equip laypeople to witness will be encouraged and rebuked when they realize that they have men, women, and youth who can and are willing to be equipped to win souls. Sunday School teachers will be encouraged when they learn Bo led one of his Sunday School class members to Christ after a few short hours of training in how to share his personal testimony and read a gospel booklet.

Some will be rebuked when they realize that they do not know the spiritual condition of many of their class members and have never tried to lead a lost person to Christ. Laypeople will be encouraged as they become aware that God can effectively use them to exhort, encourage, and equip other laypeople, pastors, missionaries, and denominational workers to be more effective soul-winners. Many others will be rebuked when they read of the heartache Bo experienced, even though he had been a Christian 19 years, when he was unable to talk about Christ in a meaningful way to his dying business partner.

It is my prayer that every person who reads this book will be inspired to follow Bo Mitchell's example in becoming a soul-winner and an equipper of others. This will result in multitudes being saved and in countless Christians experiencing great joy.

"I pray that you may be active in sharing your faith, so that you will have a full understanding of every good thing we have in Christ." (Philemon 6 NIV).

What They're Saying About
You CAN Take It with You . . .

"Bo Mitchell has a unique point of view, and I pray it will be experienced. . . ." —Richard W. Everett, Personal Evangelism, Baptist State Convention of North Carolina

"Bo has effectively and mightily been used as he leads the National CWT seminars. I believe his testimony and lifestyle lend a tremendous amount of integrity to his material." —Tim Deatrick, Associate Pastor, Tower Grove Baptist Church, Saint Louis, Missouri

"Bo's compassion and love for people, plus his gathering of materials, make his book a must to share with others." —Tom Burns, Senior Associate Pastor, Merrimon Avenue Baptist Church, Asheville, North Carolina

"After meeting Bo, being involved in his conference, and hearing about the content of this book, I prayed that the book would become a reality." —Travis Wiginton, Pastor, Kona Baptist Church, Kailua-Kona, Hawaii

"Bo, I know the Lord will continue to use you in a mighty way." —Dan Greer, Tusculum Baptist Church, Greeneville, Tennessee

1
Wings of Gold

They that go down to the sea in ships, that do business in great waters; These see the works of the Lord, and his wonders in the deep. For he commandeth, and raiseth the stormy wind, which lifteth up the waves thereof. They mount up to the heavens; and they go down against the depths; their soul is melted because of trouble. They reel to and fro, and stagger like a drunken man, and are at their wits' end (Ps. 107:23-27).

Darkness settled over a disturbed, anxious, and vast expanse of the Western Pacific. The greatest armada of fighting ships the world had ever known, the US Third Fleet, suspended refueling operations because of rough seas. Winds gradually increased. The barometer continued to fall, an ominous sign. All through the night, the pitch and roll of my ship, the *Altamaha,* a light escort carrier, steadily grew worse. Daybreak eased out of black night. The dread truth was upon us! We were trapped in the claws of one of nature's most destructive forces, a full-blown, angry typhoon. Weather forecasters could not pinpoint the storm center or indicate its path.

Admiral William "Bull" Halsey, one of World War II's toughest men, had been directing carrier plane raids against the Japanese on the island of Luzon in support of the invasion of Mindoro in the Philippines. Eight battleships, twenty carriers, and scores of smaller cruisers, destroyers, and support ships were facing a struggle for survival, a battle with nature. Some would lose. In a few days it would be Christmas 1944. Seven hundred ninety seamen would not live to see that day.

Seas churned as waves fifty, sixty, and seventy-five feet high smashed into the ships, practically submerging many. Bulkheads on the *Altamaha* creaked and groaned, stretching and straining, wrenching and twisting against the immeasurable forces of the typhoon. Sounds of destruction intensified from every direction.

Cables and lines holding planes broke loose. A plane moved across the hangar deck out of control, slamming into another and breaking it loose. The forward elevator, used to move planes from the flight deck above to the hangar deck below, stuck open. Water poured in. The sound of wind increased to the roar of a hundred jets, tearing at everything in sight. Men screamed orders trying to free the elevator. Frantic efforts were made to secure the loose aircraft, now sliding back and forth with each roll of the ship. A small crane careened crazily across the lower deck. Loudspeakers pierced the air, "The smoking lamp is out. Light no cigarettes. There is grave danger of fire and explosion. Repeat, the smoking lamp is out!" Gasoline covered the hangar deck.

As the roll increased, planes were torn loose from the flight deck above and thrown into the catwalk, a retaining area to the side of the carrier. With more weight moving to the starboard (right) side, the ship rolled and hung there before slowly coming back. It would roll, hang there, and ease back. Each roll seemed more severe than the last. My fears mounted. I knew we would either capsize or break in two, slamming into the giant seas. Smaller destroyers, dancing atop the furor, were in even worse peril. Fuel spent, they were rolling two thirds of the way over—and more. Three of them, the *Monoghan, Spence,* and *Hull,* rolled and kept rolling until they had twisted into their watery grave, carrying hundreds to their deaths.

The *Altamaha,* now with peak winds now near 125 knots or

more, rolled far to the side once more and hung for what seemed an eternity. There was crashing and snapping above as the planes in the catwalk broke loose and plummeted into the ocean. I'm not sure we would have made it through one more roll. I tried to pray. Words would not come. I was lost, no comprehension of hell or heaven. There was one concern, saving physical life. For the first time in my life I understood deadly fear and panic. *This is it. I'm going to die!* Had it not been for a fellow pilot, I would have gone berserk. His face remains, over forty years later, his name long forgotten.

By mid-afternoon the peak winds of the murderous typhoon had passed. The barometer began to rise. We had survived. Nearly eight hundred did not. They were dead or missing, and seventy-five more were injured. One-hundred-forty-five planes were blown away or damaged beyond repair. Some ships traveled thousands of miles to Pearl Harbor for repairs. A crippled Third Fleet, impotent and spent, staggered back to Ulithi Atoll to regroup and lick its wounds.

> Then they cry unto the Lord in their trouble, and he brings them out of their distresses. He maketh the storm a calm, so that the waves thereof are still. Then they are glad because they be quiet; so he bringeth them unto their desired haven. Oh that men would praise the Lord for his goodness, and for his wonderful works to the children of men! (Ps. 107:28-31).

After some days the fleet steamed again. Orders arrived, sending me to the aircraft carrier *Yorktown*. I was transferred in a bosun's chair. Secured by ropes and a pulley, the canvas chair I occupied was pulled over open water from the *Altamaha* to a destroyer while both ships steamed ahead. My transfer safely completed, the destroyer cut away and headed for the *Yorktown*. Before I could make the last transfer, seas began to boil again. *No, not this again. I can't take another typhoon. I'll have heart failure!* I was to experience another night of fear, this one not as deadly as the last, but still a hair-raiser. The destroyer rolled forty-five degrees, halfway over in the darkness. I finally made it to the *Fighting Lady,* feeling I had been in combat already. My role was that of a Navy replacement pilot, taking the place of one lost or shot down, in all probability dead.

Over the next few months I was involved in a number of raids and submarine patrols. My squadron hit Iwo Jima, Luzon, Chichi Jima, and Formosa (now Taiwan) and made the first Navy plane raids on Tokyo before leaving the battle zones for home. Stopping only briefly in Hawaii, I boarded a British aircraft carrier for San Diego.

I wept openly at the first sight of California. Years later, when I knew God personally through His Son Jesus, I thanked Him for protecting me through those dangerous and trying months in the Pacific. I could have been gone a hundred times in a split second, lost in hell. Psalm 29:1-3, 10 expresses my thoughts of Thanksgiving,

> Give unto the Lord glory and strength. Give unto the Lord the glory due unto His name; . . . The voice of the Lord is upon the waters: the God of glory thundereth; the Lord is upon many waters. The Lord sitteth upon the flood; yea, the Lord sitteth King for ever.

I was twenty-one years old.

Within a month I was in a new squadron stationed at Ream Field south of San Diego. We were to train for three months and then return overseas. Our Marines suffered staggering losses fighting their way into Okinawa. The next stop would be Japan itself. I dreaded that possibility. More men could lose their lives in that battle than in any heretofore in the Pacific.

Scottie, Guzzo, DeBaker, Wilson, Smith, Breckheiser, all became fellow pilots and friends. Their faces and names faintly focus today. We lived, flew, and played together in a setting far different from the Pacific war zones. Traveling up and down the California coast from Los Angeles to San Francisco and further, we lived it up. Guzzo and Scottie both had girl friends who visited them. They were to be married before our next overseas trip.

Amid all the excitement of flying and living the so-called good life of a Navy pilot: handsome uniforms, girls everywhere; I was a very lonely person.

Our squadron moved to the Mojave Desert in California for bomb and rocket practice. The heat was worse than in the Pacific. When not flying we were in our barracks playing poker or on leave somewhere in California. Frequent trips in our Grumman Avenger aircraft over the desert and mountains were breathtaking ventures, scenery out of storybooks. When Guzzo flew I noticed how much closer he came to the desert floor and mountains than I. His propeller seemed to mow the grass in the mountain valleys. He dodged tall cacti in the desert. I was uneasy. He would fly me to Los Angeles and cause the hair to rise on my neck because of his daring nature in the cockpit. He continually made the best scores in rocketry and bombing.

And then Guzzo was dead!

He was killed one afternoon as he swept in too low in a rocket run. Two crewmen, he, and the airplane were scattered over the desert sands. Was this always smiling, good-natured buddy really gone? I asked myself several disturbing questions. *What was life all about anyway? When we died, then what?* I brushed aside those thoughts. There would be no wedding. We were to have a funeral. We gathered for a memorial service in the desert chapel where Guzzo had worshiped while most of us had slept. We said good-bye.

Nagging questions continued to bother me. *Could there be more than this? Was there more than a beer bottle and beautiful scenery, girls, and airplanes?*

Radio news reports carried a strange story of a bomb that

wiped out two Japanese cities. Multiplied thousands had been killed in an instant!

Suddenly the war was over. All training operations ceased. We jumped into our planes and flew to San Diego, to be a part of one the most ungodly celebrations ever to hit America. I can still see thousands of sailors, some drunk out of their heads, shouting and screaming, jumping into fountains, kissing every girl in sight, and generally going crazy.

The next morning, with a terrible hangover, I slipped out of the hotel room that was filled with sleeping people. Walking alone down a street, now quiet and deserted, I knew this exciting but demanding, deadly but deeply disturbed period of my life was over.

Florida

In 1946 I returned home to Florida and enrolled at the University of Florida to study journalism. An English professor suggested I consider radio broadcasting as a career. Airplanes and wide-open seas, white uniforms, big cities all crowded into my mind as I attempted to study. To supplement my veteran's benefits I secured a job during the summer months at a land-title company office. This was more boring than college, hours and hours of pouring over small print, sitting in one place. In that office I met a lovely brunette, slender, and somewhat shy, unlike most of the girls I had known.

The local newspapers carried a story about a radio station to be built in Winter Haven. I decided to follow my English professor's advice and find a job as an announcer. The program director, Dick Eyrick, was not impressed. Holding his hands far apart above his head, he said, "Your inexperience is wide, great, a big problem."

"I can do it, I'll learn. I'll work harder than anyone else. You'll see," I insisted. Day after day I pressed him. He promised nothing. A few days before the station went on the air, he cornered me in the hallway.

"You've got a job. But first let me warn you. You'll work fifty hours a week, and the pay is only twenty-five dollars." How long can you live with that?"

My reply was quick, "I'll take it. When do we start?"

I stumbled while reading commercials, introducing records, reading newscasts, or ad-libbing. Wonder upon wonder that I wasn't fired. Soon I had a wire recorder under my arm doing man-on-the-street broadcasts. My first brush with celebrities came. I interviewed Esther Williams and Peter Lawford who were making a movie at Cypress Gardens, even then the water-ski capital of the world. My first play-by-play broadcasts of football games were confusing. Listeners were in the dark most of the time. I was terrible, but I was learning.

Dates with the brunette, Mickie, began. After working the late shift at the radio station, I'd take a cab to her rooming house, meet her on the porch for an hour, and take another cab home. Matters became serious when I spent more money on taxis than I was earning!

A preacher from one of the local churches had a weekly radio broadcast; and we visited each time he came in. I listened to his programs but never once did he ask about my spiritual condition. I had no real idea what Christianity was all about. I continued in my lost condition.

He performed the ceremony as Mickie and I were married June 10, 1948. She, her mother, and I decorated the small church. We borrowed two-hundred dollars from a small loan company and went to Hollywood, Florida, on our honeymoon. My father gave us a small mobile home as a wedding present.

I grew up in a small, tin-roofed house as an orange-grove caretaker's son, I was determined to make it in broadcasting. I twisted my radio dial from station to station when not working, searching for new ideas. My fingers kept going back to a

station in Orlando, WORZ. All the announcers sounded professional. One day I called their program director with a blunt
statement. "I want to go to work for you." Jack Rathbun
laughed, "How about that! We're looking for another announcer. Come on up and audition." All the long hours, the reading,
the on-the-street work, and the sports play-by-play paid off. I
was hired. So began the next step in my search for fame and
fortune. My salary was fifty dollars per week and I worked only
forty-five hours!

Tougher days in our marriage were on the horizon. I tried
to attend Rollins College in the daytime and work a night shift.
Not many months later our first son was born. A crying baby
claimed center stage. I quit school.

My boss moved to Pensacola. He called one evening to tell
me he had recommended me as program director in a radio
station there. With his help I got the job. The next step in the
treasure hunt was completed. My salary was seventy-five dollars a week.

It was 1950. We were to live in Pensacola—the cradle of
naval aviation—for seventeen years, where in 1944 I had received my wings of gold. In my wildest dreams I never thought
I'd return. I became more consumed with my work, grinding
away day and night—more hours, more responsibility than ever
before. Mickie started going to church. It didn't interest me,
there were too many other things to do—fishing, working, and
working some more. I noted that sales personnel in the station
made more money than I, so I began to call on businesses part
time. We moved into a larger rental house on the outskirts of
town. We bought a building lot next door, and my father came
to help me construct a house. A second child was on the way.
Each night he and I labored till midnight.

My dad had been born in Bulgaria and had come to America
as a young man. The drive in my soul was inherited from
him. He told of life as a teenage boy when he many times slept
in the fields with cattle. Nothing was so important to him as

"getting ahead," saving money, and having a home, looking to no one. Neither he nor my mother were churchgoers.

We moved into our new home with our two sons, Gary and Ron.

On November 13, 1956, I was to celebrate my thirty-third birthday. The day began like most Sundays. Mickie and the boys made ready for Sunday School and church. I was going fishing. Right before walking out the door, I looked back at the three of them, turned, and said, "I'll go with you today." They were shocked. This wasn't really Bo. Many times before, Gary had asked why I wouldn't go with them. I had never given him a satisfactory answer.

We went to an early service at First Baptist Church, Pensacola. Dr. Nathan Brooks preached a sermon entitled "Promises and Demands." The first part sounded OK, this wonderful country God had given us, the unchanging promises of God, love of family, and so forth. I related to that. Dr. Brooks moved to demands, and I became edgy. This wasn't for me. At the end of the service I told Mickie I'd see her later and walked out of the church and down the hill. Half a block away I turned to see Dr. Brooks standing on the steps and realized in that instant I had run from God for thirty-three years. All those questions that flooded my mind years ago were answered that morning: *Why we are here? Where are we going? What is life?*

Returning, I shook his hand and said, "You had a good sermon this morning. It was very meaningful." Being sensitive to people's needs he said, "Let's visit in my study before the next service. Let's talk about it." A few minutes later I was on my knees asking Jesus to forgive me and be my Savior! Dr. Brooks eased out to call Mickie.

"Don't bother her. She's in Bible study," I answered.

"I'm sure she'd like to know about this," he exclaimed. She came in crying. So did her teacher, Mrs. Mose Penton, and a number of young ladies in the class. They had been praying on my behalf for years!

2
Fool's Gold

Be ever on the alert and always on your guard against every form of greed, because a man's life does not consist in his possessions, even though they are abundant (Luke 12:15, Williams).

Better is little with the fear of the Lord than great treasure and trouble therewith (Prov. 15:16).

I became deeply involved in the life of the church right away. It was easy since Mickie was already a part of the fellowship. My Sunday School class took me under its wing. When I was absent, one of the men called. We painted classrooms, went on picnics and outings with our families, studied the Bible, and attended worship services together. They were a caring group. Someone asked me to assume a small responsibility with the class. I did, and other tasks came my way. Mickie and I were attending church on Sunday morning and Sunday night, plus Wednesday evening prayer meeting. Two years later I was asked to be a deacon. There were also committee assignments. I was busy, busy, busy.

Yet, one of the dread tragedies of my Christian walk was occurring. I learned nothing about sharing Christ! Oh, I heard some talk about "The Roman Road." But no one really seemed interested in witnessing. I began to broadcast local high-school football games. On Sunday morning, or at any other time, conversation centered on last Friday night's game, or the latest juicy news broadcast. In fact it would be nineteen years from the day I accepted Christ until I made my first witnessing visit! How many will go to hell or are already there because I didn't learn to share? There's the salesman who worked for me, the announcer, both long since dead. I was able to meet people everywhere, store owners and businessmen by the score, neighbors, fishing partners, and many others. I was as well known as the most popular politician in the area, but my mouth was closed when it came to speaking about Jesus.

My search for "fool's gold" continued. I had to make that million dollars. Ten- to twelve-hour workdays were the norm. I was busy in civic activities, president of the West Florida Heart Association, a member of the board of directors of Baptist Hospital and the Pensacola Sports Association, and sponsor of the Pensacola Open, a major PGA golf tournament. Our radio broadcast crews followed Arnold Palmer, Doug Sanders, Doug Ford, Gary Player, and others. I talked to and interviewed golfing's greats. This pattern of burning the candle in the middle and at both ends went on and on.

One day I found myself in my doctor's office skirting the edge of a nervous breakdown. He asked me to make a list of all my civic responsibilities, church assignments, and vocational tasks. He returned, took the list, and began to cross through a number of my entries, saying, "This can be done by some retiree with nothing else to do. Forget this one. You've got to let up in your work. That radio station will be there long after you're dead. Either you make some changes, or we may bury you one day soon." Temporarily shocked, I walked out asking the right questions. Where was I really headed? I might not make the million. In fact I might not make anything! Pride moved in to assume residence more strongly than ever. Prestige, a grasp for the impossible, drove me day after day. Nothing would stop me.

Since my father helped me build our first house, we were now able to put aside money every payday. Getting deeper in sales and sales management, I made more and more money each month. By 1961 Mickie and I had saved ten thousand dollars. We wore very simple clothes, drove an old car, and bought only what we needed.

Early that year I received a telephone call from the new owner of the oldest and most prestigious radio station in the city. He suggested, "I'd like to meet with you soon. I think I have something you'll really be interested in." During our first conference he told me he had reserved 12 percent of the stock in the station for his station manager. He added, "You're my man. I'm offering you the job." I asked how much it would take to purchase the stock. His reply, "Ten thousand dollars." Aha! Just the amount we had saved, to the penny. Within days the deal was struck, and I moved on in my grand plan, now as part owner and manager. Before leaving, the wife of my dear friend, Don Lynch, a man I had worked for ten years, admonished me, "I'm not sure you'll fit into what you're up to in the long run. Greed doesn't wear well on you." Those words came back to haunt me years later. At the time I brushed aside her remarks, even as I had my doctor's.

Pushing ahead full steam, I carried a number of faithful employees with me. After an initial time of struggle, we were on our way. For the next few years success seemed to move with my every step. My personal income continued to rise. We had the hottest property in town.

Another event occurred in 1963 that was to feed my pride enormously. I auditioned for the role of play-by-play announcer for the Florida State University football network and won the job. Now, in addition to everything else I was involved in, I traveled all over the country as part of something I never dreamed possible. In my first broadcast, Florida State played the University of Miami in Orange Bowl Stadium. Telegrams of encouragement poured in following a game packed with excitement and suspense. Florida State won going away after a young defensive back intercepted a Miami pass and ran it back ninety-nine yards for a touchdown. Fred Biletnikoff would become an All-American on offense. He was destined to play for the Oakland Raiders for years and became a superstar, playing in the Super Bowl, as an All-Pro and in 1988 was named to NFL Hall of Fame. I traveled with the team as FSU played Alabama, Georgia, Florida, North Carolina State, Miami, Syracuse, Baylor, and other tough football schools. I became friends with Vaughn Mancha, athletic director of Florida State. He had been an All-American at Alabama during his playing days. He was also one of the most honorable men I met during my ten years of college football broadcasting. The crowds, the stars, the whole scene seemed unreal; surely it was a fairy tale. I later won the "Sportscaster of the Year" award for the state of Florida, chosen by fellow broadcasters and sportswriters. Attending the national award ceremonies in North Carolina, I met Paul Dietzel who had coached LSU to a national championship in football, Jim Murray, renowned sportswriter for *The Los Angeles Times,* Chris Schenkle of ABC Television Sports, and other nationally known celebrities. I was part of the play-by-play team to broadcast the first Fiesta Bowl worldwide. Over the years I did a number of other bowl broadcasts.

Three wonderful children, a lovely faithful Christian wife, money coming in like water to a poor country boy and a certain amount of fame to go with the good fortune—what more could a guy want in this life?

Occasionally a nagging question surfaced: *What would be the effect in eternity of this fame, fortune, and sports broadcasting?*

In 1964 the tides of fortune continued to roll. One of my partners invited me to invest in a radio station he was buying with others in Orlando. Was I interested? I practically climbed over the desk in my enthusiasm! An option was secured, we borrowed $350,000 from a Chicago bank, and closed the deal. It was April 1965. One month later Walt Disney announced he would build Disney World in Orlando. The value of our property doubled overnight! We had hardly lifted a finger. A lot of breaks had come my way but surely this would be the biggest yet.

In less than two years, Mickie, our three sons, Gary, Ron, and Brad, and I left Pensacola for Orlando. I went to assist one of my partners who was very ill. His activity was restricted and the prognosis was not promising. In fact, he was dying. There was no hope of recovery. We became very close. I was his eyes and ears in the business. We met daily at his home on a nearby lake. His wife prepared lunch while we visited by the pool. Conversations ran the gamut, from business to politics, on to family, and finally to spiritual matters. I found myself trying to put words of assurance together. I asked timid questions about his relationship to God. Words came but they failed to accomplish what I hoped for. I groped. In his gracious way he assured me all was well.

But, I was still troubled. Why couldn't I talk about Christ in a meaningful way? Here was a man approaching his greatest hour of need and I was no real help. This was where I needed to call upon great spiritual resources. I had no idea how to do so. As I suffered with him through those last months of his life, I realized I had been too occupied making money and seeking fame to take time to follow closely by the Lord. I had been busy in church and with a thousand other things. What I termed *success* had failed me.

Tom died about one o'clock in the morning as I sat by his hospital bed with a nurse. No one else was in the room. He reached out as his breathing slowed, we took him by the hand, and he gently moved into eternity. I was called on to select his casket and make arrangements at the funeral home. I wondered if I would ever see him again.

From that day forward I determined to know more about the person of Christ Himself. It was no longer enough to attend worship services, or deacons' meetings, or the other things busy church people attend. Surely there was more.

3
Discovery

He said to them, "Come! Follow me, and I will make you
fishermen for catching men." And at once they left their nets
and followed Him. (Matt. 4:19-20, (Williams).

Glistening gold chains, looped and folded around his neck,
covered a black leather vest. Into the pulpit he stepped at First
Baptist Church in Orlando. Completely unconventional, this
character declared that witnessing meant lovingly confronting
people anywhere, everywhere. When he gave his account of
stopping prostitutes on the sidewalk in Hollywood, California
and talking Jesus to them, even leading some to make a commitment, I said to myself, "Hold on now Lord. This guy's a nut.
He's making up these tales. I don't believe him." As Arthur
Blessit continued to weave his stories, I remembered some of
my fellow church members had talked about witnessing. Some
became so interested they were making radical commitments to
go to the foreign mission field!

Because of the long illness and death of my partner in Orlando, the radio station there was sold. My share of the profit was
two-hundred thousand dollars, not bad for an investment of
ten-thousand dollars over a period of six years. Hardly pausing
to catch our breath, my remaining partner and I purchased a
station in Bradenton, Florida. My family and I moved again,
this time to sun, sea, and sands; the Asolo Theatre nearby, golf

courses galore, churches everywhere, and what promised to be a continuation of the good life. We were becoming Florida gypsies. What a wonderful way to be a gypsy. This had to be near-Paradise.

For the first time we began to travel extensively. We bought a large motor home and drove ten thousand miles through the West into the Canadian Rockies, down the coast to San Francisco, and back home across the heart of America. Off to Europe we went, to Paris, London, Rome, and Madrid. Was this really the poor boy raised on a orange grove in a tin-roof house, now gazing at Michelangelo's timeless treasures in the Sistine Chapel in Rome, attending the theater in London, walking the wide boulevards and small side streets in Paris, listening and staring as bullfighters crazed the crowds in Madrid?

Returning from Europe, I was called to Augusta, Georgia, to consider our next station purchase. I listened to all the details and looked over the documents. There were serious reservations in my mind. I said to my prospective partners, "We're giving too much. The present owner is getting a huge salary guarantee, the price looks inflated, we get no property, and frankly it just doesn't add up. I don't believe we'll ever be able to pay all this." I was told this was the best deal possible, take it or leave it. Instead of listening to that small voice of caution inside, the desire to make that million dollars overshadowed all reason. After all, hadn't everything we touched turned to gold for the last ten years? I signed the papers. My personal liability exceeded six-hundred thousand dollars.

The high flying continued. My radio network broadcasts, sponsored by a major oil company, were doing well. Our Pensacola station was making money. The new Bradenton property was emerging from years of neglect and our basic plan of bringing new life to sick radio stations was successful. I played golf with fellow businessmen, became a member of the board of directors of the largest local bank, and continued to attend church regularly. I had been a deacon for fifteen years and would now serve on the active body at West Bradenton Baptist Church.

A plea for an injection of funds came from our partner in Augusta. This was temporary, the start-up was more difficult than he thought, but everything was moving in the right direction. We'd be out of the woods in no time.

Mickie and I taught a married young couples class in Sunday School and began to forge friendships that would last through eternity. When we left Pensacola, I felt we'd never find another church I'd really like. We found new Christian friends in Orlando. Now there were new friends in Bradenton. The deacon body elected me as chairman, and later I was to serve as chairman of the pastor-search committee. The months eased into years.

Periodically, calls for more money came from Augusta. They became more frequent. It wasn't long until I used most of my profits from the Orlando sale feeding this money-hungry giant. We sold the Pensacola station in 1975 for nearly six times the 1961 purchase price. My first ten-thousand-dollar investment made a profit of over two-hundred thousand. Augusta was a temporary setback on the road to the million, or so I thought! I was finding it more and more difficult to convince myself. As the Augusta station neared bankruptcy, one of the partners decided to restructure the debt and bring in local talent to change direction. My stock was needed to complete the plan. Since I considered it worthless, I wrote off the loss and felt happy to bail out. The only problem—I wasn't out. My name remained on the primary notes, now over six-hundred thousand dollars.

The most significant event of my Christian life this side of salvation was about to occur. Mickie and I were invited to attend a Lay Evangelism School in our church. After three evening class sessions, everyone went visiting to put into practice what had been learned. My visitation partner was a young lady in the Sunday School class Mickie and I taught. Jan and I knocked on the first door. No one was at home. The same thing happened at the second door. I commented to Jan, "Let's make it three for three." Sure enough—no answer there either. *Let's get back to the church and see what everyone is doing* was my first thought. Out came the words. But the young lady had other ideas, "Why don't we go see somebody?" Slightly embarrassed that I hadn't come up with the idea, I agreed.

We decided to visit a couple who hadn't been to Sunday School for awhile, and knocked on Phil's door. After explaining to him what we were about, I asked if I could share my brief testimony. He nodded, "Go ahead." Out came the two-minute, condensed version, concluding with the question, "Has anything like this ever happened to you?" He sat quietly for a moment, looked up, and answered, "No it hasn't."

Shock came over me. He had been a member of our class for two years. I didn't have the spiritual sensitivity to suspect he was lost. Stumbling for words, I reached in my pocket and pulled out a witnessing booklet; "Would you let me read this to you?" With his permission I presented it word for word. Concluding, I explained if he'd give all to God, ask Jesus to forgive him and be his Savior, God would do for him what he did for me years ago. My hand trembled holding the booklet as he prayed. Astonished and dumbfounded, I couldn't believe what had happened. It couldn't be this easy—no fighting, coercing, pushing!

We returned to the church and found others with the same experience. One led to Christ had been a member of our class before he and his wife went away to the university. He never said a word back in those days, always troubled. He had a great need, the need for salvation, and we were unable to minister to him or witness. Bob Dring and his wife Karen would become two of our dearest friends. As we prepared to go home, Gerald Hooker, our teacher for the week, asked if he could visit our youngest son, Brad. We arranged the meeting at our home. Gerald came at 11 PM. As Mickie and I sat in another part of the house, questions crowded my mind. *Did this man really care so much for others that he would visit at midnight? How could one be so unselfish?*

A few months later Hooker called to invite me to go as his prayer partner to Cali, Colombia, in South America. Eighteen other laymen and their pastor from North Central Church in Gainesville, Florida were going to teach lay evangelism schools in ten churches and mission points in that great city of a million people. God had really gotten my attention in the first lay evangelism school. I felt there was much more.

We arrived in Cali near midnight after traveling most of the day. I collapsed on a small cot at the Baptist seminary where we were housed. Just before I fell asleep, one of the men stuck his head in the door, "Let's go to the chapel for a prayer meeting." *My stars* I thought, *a prayer meeting this time of night.* "Lord You must have something important to say." There in the chapel these laypersons and their pastor got on their knees, some on their faces, one after another praying, "Lord we know You want us to tell others about You this week. You want us to teach. Lord whatever You desire us to do, we're willing. We are Your servants. Lord, use us so that it pleases You." Some wept. It went on for over an hour. Returning to my room I realized I had never been in a prayer meeting comparable to this one.

The next day I gave my testimony in the seminary chapel while the others went across the city to preach. Monday afternoon we went into the city. Walking along, I noticed our men stopping to engage total strangers in conversation. Here and there they took out Spanish tracts and encouraged the Colombians themselves to read. After observing for a short time I decided to try. Approaching a young man sitting on the curb I attempted the few words of Spanish I knew and reached for my tract. "Fellow, I'm from Brooklyn. You don't have to struggle so," he chuckled. About halfway through the tract, I called to Gerald for help. For the first time I tried to witness to a total stranger. God had moved me across another of the barriers Satan builds, the barrier of "No stranger will talk to you about Jesus."

Our group had two assignments. One was to work on the roof of a small church during the day and the other to teach lay evangelism schools at night, using an interpreter. Hooker and I went to a church pastored by Harold Garcia. His wife, Diane, was to interpret for Hooker. The second evening nine teenage boys came into the small sanctuary after we started. Harold moved to the side to talk to them while the teaching continued. He motioned to me and said, "Give your testimony." After I finished he presented the gospel to all nine. In a circle with our arms around them, the nine prayed one by one and accepted Christ! So amazed and stunned I could not speak, I prayed silently, "Oh, Lord, where have I been all these years? I'm seeing laypersons, students, professors, preachers, young and old, all witnessing for You everywhere, in the church, on the street corners. Some are simple, others learned. All move with boldness. Oh God, is this what You've been trying to show me all these years?"

Revival broke out in the ten teaching points. During our five days there, 243 souls were saved. It began with a group of laymen willing to pay their own way across a continent to speak the name of Jesus to those of a different culture and language. Their pastor, Dr. N. V. Langford, preached to our group twice during the week. Other than that he had very little to do. The laymen knew what to do. And they did it. He had discipled and equipped them well! Paul, writing to Timothy in his Second Letter, stated what pastors must do if their people are to step out for Jesus. He said, "The things you learned from me before many witnesses you must commit to trustworthy men who will be competent to teach others too" (2 Tim. 2:2 Williams).

Each day we returned to the seminary for lunch. Many of the professors, teachers, and staff were full-time missionaries for the Southern Baptist Convention. Following our noon meal with them the third day, the visiting laypersons shared. One after another, they told how God was working in their lives. One would share, pause, wipe away a tear, share more, and stand silently with head bowed. An obviously poor man said, "I was able to come on this trip because a man in our church back home learned I didn't have the money. He stayed home and gave me his money so I could come. How selfish am I, here watching God at work, a part of what He is up to, and my brother is at home." Another praised God in the midst of adversity because of what God was teaching him! These were laughing, crying, praying, working, witnessing, suffering, and experiencing joy together. I believe each had decided long ago nothing in life was more important than Jesus. They were living that decision.

Next day the missionaries shared. I pictured missionaries as holy and near perfect with no deep problems or needs. I heard confessions, pleadings, calls on the Lord for intercession, blessing, salvation for others, and expressions of praise and thanksgiving. God met us mightily during those days. I had been a Christian for nearly twenty years. The depth of what I was seeing and where God was leading was frightening!

Gerald and I stopped in Bogotá on our way back to Miami. We walked the crowded streets handing out tracts and taking pictures. There had been recent unrest in Colombia. Soldiers were everywhere. Two approached, rifles on their shoulders. Gerald, smiled, shook hands with them, and handed each a tract. They nodded and walked away, reading. At the end of one street we were surrounded by ten to fifteen children. Ragged clothes were falling off their backs. Shivering, a few held small plastic bags containing all they owned. Some were pitiful, some tough, but more gathered as we handed out coins, bills, and tracts till there were none left. These were the street children of Bogotá—no home, no place to stay warm, no school, no one to care, abandoned, some six years old, fighting for a piece of bread. God impressed my heart that Jesus cared. He cared as much for these homeless children as for anyone else in the whole world.

On our way home, thousands of feet over the Caribbean, I prayed, "Lord I haven't begun to understand all You've shown me during these days. I know You've been with me every step of the way. You've spoken. You've empowered laypeople as I've never seen before. It's been a miracle to me! Lord, I don't want to waste the rest of my life chasing after money and fame. Lord, I want to be more like these men and these missionaries and most of all, more like You!"

Jesus reached down where most of us live when he spoke these words in the Sermon on the Mount,

> Stop storing up your riches on earth where moths and rust make away with them, and where thieves break in and steal them. But keep on storing up your riches in heaven where moths and rust do not make away with them and where thieves do not break in and steal them. For wherever your treasure is, there too your heart will be (Matt. 6:19-21, Williams).

God had used a group of ordinary men—a laborer, shirt salesman, a motel manager, insurance salesman, photographer, others—to show men hearts and lives sold out to Him!

"Jim, how does one get equipped to teach lay evangelism schools? I believe God wants me to do that." That was how I introduced myself on the phone to Jim Ponder, then evangelism director of Florida Baptists. After a few questions he invited me to leadership witness training at Baptist Bible Institute in Graceville, Florida, adding, "You can come if you pay your own way." I was to relive some of the experiences of Cali. Two hundred students moved out over the countryside and towns of northwest Florida and scores were saved, all directed to the local churches. Another blessing God showered on me was fellowship with Ponder and Max Cadenhead, his associate. Their lives were filled with the power of God. I was enthralled. They became two of my dearest friends and brothers in Christ in the months and years ahead. Every few months Ponder would let me lead a witnessing school in Florida. Everywhere I saw people come to Christ, as laymen with simple, basic training, stepped out in faith and shared, most for the first time.

The year turned into 1977 as the hustle and bustle of radio broadcasting continued. But the edge was no longer there. As I worked to solve business problems my mind wandered back to Cali, Graceville, Bogotá, to Gerald, Jim, Max, and the others. After being consumed by an electronic marvel for over thirty years, I knew it was over. I decided to sell the Bradenton radio station, not knowing for sure what God had in store. Mickie was very surprised when I told her about the decision. "What will you do," she asked? "You'll never believe this. But, I'm convinced God wants me to get involved in His work in some way maybe even full time," I answered. We prayed. Doubts crowded my mind. I wasn't prepared for a ministry, no college degree, no seminary training, just a layperson. I put out a "fleece," "Lord if this radio station sells, I'll know You're in it."

After only a few weeks an offer came at exactly the asking price! Before I could sign the contract another offer arrived. I had my answer, two times over.

While visiting with Ponder one day, he shot a question to me, "Why don't you come work with Max and me, full-time in personal evangelism? You can teach witnessing schools in Florida." Everything came into sharp focus. The radio-station sale was completed. Much of my share of the profit was in long-term notes. I had an income for fifteen years. In addition, another investment, made a few years earlier, began to pay handsome dividends. Three oil and gas leases near a large field in northwest Florida became productive. There was enough income to last the rest of our lives. We became Mission Service Corps volunteers and were assigned to Ponder's department in Florida.

God used Jim to open door after door in our lives. We saw the miracle of salvation come alive in lost people all over the state, people witnessed to by laypersons, simple men and women using testimony and Scripture.

Every few months rumors told of more trouble in Augusta. But, my partner had sold the station to others with considerable financial resources; they would handle the problem one way or another. Like a thorn in the flesh, the haunting dark cloud would not go away. When I prayed, I would say something like this, "Lord I've turned from everything else and placed all in Your hands. You've given us the money to use serving You. Everything is just the way it ought to be. Don't let it change." Instead of asking God for direction, I was trying to give Him direction. If I had listened, I'm sure He would have said, "I'm capable of deciding what to do and accomplishing it." I had to help God along!

When not traveling, Mickie and I remained deeply involved in the outreach ministry of our local church. We were to see real revival in the months just ahead. A new pastor, Bob Allen from Ormand Beach, had been called. He told all the deacons and their wives before he came, reaching lost people would be his first priority and if we called him, we must be a part of that ministry. For the first couple of months he went out and knocked on doors everywhere, many times alone. First one, then another began to walk down the aisle making professions of faith Sunday mornings. He called me one day and stated,

"We're going to have a lay evangelism school and I want you to help me teach. No excuses; you help me."

On the first night we expected fifty or possibly sixty members to attend; one-hundred and eighty people showed up! Fever-pitch excitement began to take place in the church. Some had prayed for years for revival. Our deacons' meetings turned into prayer meetings and times of thanksgiving. On Sunday mornings the deacons would line up on the sides of the sanctuary and begin to pray and weep. The lost and those making public decisions came. The invitation went on, no way to stop with people coming! Laymen witnessed all week, led by Allen. Always people came down the aisles! The previous year we baptized thirteen. During the first twelve months of Allen's ministry close to two hundred were baptized. Month after month, year after year it continued. The Sunday School more than doubled in attendance from four-hundred to nine-hundred in a five-year period. Eight hundred were baptized. It truly became a sweeping harvest of souls.

Bob called me one Saturday morning, "I'll be by with Bob Dring in about an hour. Go with us to visit the Grants down the street from you." I was ready. We were warmly received by this family of eight plus a teenage visitor. Eleven of us sat in a circle around Allen who took his place on the floor. He talked to the children for a few minutes, asked the parents some questions, and presented the gospel. When decision time came, he sent Dring into the den with one, I went to the kitchen with another, and he counseled with another. One by one all nine made professions of faith! In the midst of my elation, God said, "You live less than a block away. These were lost and you did not go to them. Why?" "Why" is the great question God is asking the Christian church today. And we provide no satisfactory answer, only feeble excuses. Isaiah said, "I heard the voice of the Lord, saying, Whom shall I send, and who will go for us?" Isaiah answered, "Here am I; send me" (Isa. 6:8). God continues to call.

Bold, brash Bob Allen went, wasted no time, and presented Jesus to the Grants. Everyone was saved. All were baptized and became active members of the church. He, Howard Ramsey, and Jim Ponder were destined to be role-model witnesses in my life!

4
Exotic Island Treasure

Never stop praying (1 Thes. 5:17, Williams).

More things are wrought by prayer than this world dreams of
—(Alfred, Lord Tennyson).

Excitement rose when we contemplated a visit to an exotic island in the Caribbean. I opened an invitation to accompany Jim Ponder to Jamaica. The excitement began. This was to be the first of four witness-training journeys to that tropical island, a vacation paradise for many North Americans.

We were met at the Kingston airport by Azariah McKenzie, whose work encompassed a large area of the Caribbean. As we weaved through the streets of Kingston, glaring graffiti, some repulsive, jumped out at us. McKenzie explained it was left from a recent, bitter political campaign. A leading Jamaican pastor later told me had it not been for deep Christian influence and concern during that election, the country might have plunged into radical socialism or communism.

Warm and friendly, exemplifying life and the Word, Azariah drove us northward toward the highlands. The cutting edge of poverty was evident. Small shacks, scant protection from the elements, were sprinkled across the hills. Here and there were breadfruit trees, sugarcane fields, and banana plantations. Jamaicans walked the roadside with heavy burdens perfectly balanced on their head. We stopped to enjoy tropical fruit from roadside vendors. Ponder's friendliness with the nationals always moved ultimately to Christ!

Late that afternoon we arrived at Monique. A large school had been rented for a week of Bible study, discipleship, and witness training. Four hundred Jamaicans greeted us! Jim's conversation with one or another never seemed to stop. They considered him with fascination. Rotund and jovial, his wide, loving smile gained entry into every heart.

We met the entire group each evening in a large building with a roof and cement floor but no sides, truly an outdoor setting. Our first two days passed without incident as we shared teaching assignments and had fellowship with many of the four hundred. We learned what it meant to be a minority. We two were the only whites. All the rest were black. I experienced the warmth of real Christian love as these dedicated Jamaicans treated us as one of their own.

The third morning Jim and I went sightseeing across the hills to Ocho Rios on the northern coast. The man who gave us a ride pointed out the old homeplace of Peter Lord's family. For many years he has been a rather unorthodox, but very effective Baptist pastor on the east coast of Florida. As we approached the sea, large modern hotels came into view. This was a world apart from Monique. Swimming pools, beaches, shops with colorful native crafts, and fine restaurants were everywhere. *Could we find lunch other than boiled bananas or breadfruit?* As we prepared to eat our luscious looking meal of fruit, shrimp salad, and dessert, Jim expressed an earnest prayer of thanksgiving. Two waiters standing nearby listened. One moved near and said, "You're the first person I've seen give thanks all the time I've worked here." That was all the opening Jim needed. He talked to him about Jesus.

We did not seek him out. God opened an inquisitive heart. Jim simply responded. So it was with Nicodemus. He came searching. Jesus responded. If our goal as Christians is to be more like Jesus, we must be sensitive always to those around us. God is busy preparing a receptive heart for you, another for me.

After lunch we strolled the streets for an hour or so before seeking a ride back to Monique. We found a small taxi. The driver was short, rather fat, gregarious, and boisterous. He was sweating profusely as he loaded one after another into the small vehicle. I wanted to climb out but was too embarrassed to do so. Soon I wished I had. He roared his engine as the last passenger climbed into the lap of a front-seat occupant. Up the mountain road we went, tires screeching at every turn, taking half the road and more, missing cars by inches, and generally blazing away on straightaways. To top it off, Jamaicans drive on the left side of the road. Jim and I prayed and prayed more as he fired the missile with seven souls across the hills. The driver could see our ashen faces in his rearview mirror. He smiled, turned, and asked, "Afraid?" "Yes," I yelled and prayed on! God delivered us.

On the fourth afternoon hundreds were sent out across the hills to share testimony and Scripture. Report time lasted for hours. Many were saved by many who had never before tried to witness! Since we had no classes that evening, Ponder preached at a nearby church. He asked me to share my testimony. Afterward I moved to the back of the small worship area. A group of teenagers stood, looking in. Since they would not enter, I went out and shared with two of them. One was receptive and received Christ as Savior. The other rejected Him.

Words of witness can be given in the church house, outside, in classrooms, across the neighborhood, in houses, at work, on the streets, by laypersons, preachers, men, women, youngsters, anywhere and everywhere as God opens the door. The early disciples were thrown into prison, beaten, and warned to keep quiet about Jesus. Led by Peter, they rejoiced and witnessed! The world could not shut them up.

So they went out from the presence of the council, rejoicing that they had been considered worthy to suffer disgrace for Jesus' name; and not for a single day did they stop teaching in the temple square and in private houses the good news of Jesus the Christ (Acts 5:41-42, Williams).

The very next verse tells of the disciples increasing! Want to know how to grow your church? Go and gossip Jesus as the disciples did! There is no great risk of being beaten and thrown in jail in the United States, yet.

As our week neared an end, with tongue in cheek I chided Jim for failing to preach to the four hundred. He said, "I've thought about doing just that Friday night." I laughed, "You've been thinking about this for months. You prepared a sermon long before we left Florida." On Friday the schedule turned to shambles. Cooks ran out of food. Classes were re-scheduled. It was close to 9 PM when we began our last hour of instruction. I felt sure everyone would leave by 10 o'clock. They did not. Jim moved to the makeshift pulpit and God's message poured out in power and clarity. Finishing, he challenged the still full house at 10:45, "If you're willing to take what God has taught you this week and use it to disciple others and be a witness, right there beside your chair, tell God about it."

As the chairs moved all began to pray aloud. The sound became louder and louder. The leaders looked with some sur-prise. I looked at them and back at the crowd. It seemed the roof of the building might rise at any moment! That quiet, small Voice said, "Why do you watch? And don't you know you need to pray?" I joined. How long it lasted I don't know. One of the men climbed on a table and led in a chorus. The praying stopped and a crescendo of song filled the tropical night across the countryside.

Sleep was difficult. Faintly, through a window slightly ajar, sounds awakened us at 4:30 AM. From one direction came songs and praises, from another prayers, and from still another weeping as these soul-stirred people called upon God to bring revival to Jamaica. Many had stayed up all night. A year later we were to see results because of these warriors of prayer.

Montego Bay

Our second trip to Jamaica came a few months later. Zeph Dawns, a man then in his sixties, gentle of spirit and with a deep love for people, drove us along the coastal highway east of Montego Bay. We met fifty for ongoing witness training in a rather austere setting. We fought mosquitoes at night. Bunk-style cots and cold water made us appreciate home.

These people knew great portions of Scripture by heart. As we taught they would follow aloud every time we quoted the Word, never having to open a Bible. I learned on my first trip these were praying people. Now they proved to be people of the Word. Any witness training worthy of the name includes actual witnessing. After our instruction sessions, we set out across the hills and into a nearby village to share. The young lady I drew as one of my partners stopped the first person she came to, a man in his twenties, not two-hundred yards from the retreat. He listened, watching her every move, as she drew a simple diagram demonstrating Christ's love, at the same time quoting Scripture to him. No struggle, no debate, when she asked if he would like to receive eternal life, he said, "Yes!" A willing witness, equipped, and empowered by the Holy Spirit, brings the lost to Christ. Philip, a layperson, met the Ethiopian eunuch by the roadside and explained the Scriptures to him. This young lady met a fellow Jamaican by the roadside and explained Scripture to him. Was there joy and fulfillment and victory? The eunuch went on his way rejoicing after receiving salvation. So did the Jamaican. Philip was so Spirit-filled he continued to preach and witness in all the cities on the way to Caesarea. The lady with us begged, "Oh, let me try again, please."

Another enthusiastic girl walked into a nearby bar. The bartender, noticing how lovely she was, clasped his hands together, and asked, "What I can do for you, baaybeee?", not expecting to hear about Jesus. But he did.

Winston Clementson, Jamaican evangelism director, invited Ponder and me to spend a couple of days in his home before returning to the States. We drove east of Ocho Rios to pick up one of his children. It was near dusk as we began a trek across the spine of the island on winding, potholed roads. Winston snored in the backseat as his wife muscled the old car toward home. We expected a short trip. Six hours later we arrived. As always, the warmth of Christian fellowship pushed aside any unpleasantries. The house was filled with a group of men from Mississippi who had come to assist in construction work at one of the churches. There was no running water, the town pumps had been inoperative for months. Baths were meager.

Leaving Clementson's home with time to spare, we left for the Montego Bay airport. The old car wouldn't run with an empty radiator. Stopping for water every few miles, we arrived at the airport just as the plane was scheduled to leave. We missed it. We rented a comfortable room with bath, went to one of the fine restaurants especially tuned to the desires of tourists, and relaxed.

Montego Bay Again

One year after our initial visit to the island we returned with ninety-eight pastors, laymen, and their wives. Jim flew to Kingston with fifty and I went with the other forty-eight to Montego Bay. Because of a snafu, my group had to wait over an hour at the airport for our hosts. Strolling through the waiting area, I saw clusters of people, including two or three from our group in each cluster. Eight people were led to Christ while we waited!

We moved throughout the island, joining those we had initially trained and others they had discipled. I arrived far into the countryside at ten o'clock that night. Twenty of the faithful were waiting in the small church where I was to serve. They had prayed while they waited.

After our morning prayer meeting, we left in teams of two or three. My partners were two ladies, worlds apart in means, yet close as sisters in Christ. Moving off the gravel road we walked a muddy path toward a fellow member's house. A man approached, leading a cow. The women exchanged greetings and told him they had come to visit him and his wife. He turned and led the cow, plus the three of us, up a steep slope to his house. Raindrops splattered on the tin roof as we joined his wife on a small porch. The older lady gave her testimony to the husband and said, "Has anything like that ever happened to you?" He said no. She continued, "Then I know, I just know you'll let me tell you how it could happen." A few minutes later, the old man prayed and ask God to give him life as only God could give. His wife began to weep, "You'll never know how long I've prayed for this."

Bob Vickery, a layperson from Orlando, Florida led the outreach in a nearby church. He drew a crowd in Montego Bay as we waited for our plane. He told of leading sixteen souls to Christ in one day!

Over twenty-five hundred people were saved during our four-day weekend of witnessing, preaching, and going!

On the plane, homeward bound the next morning, I sat by a well-dressed man in his fifties. We began talking soon after takeoff. He was headed for Miami to take delivery of a new sailing vessel. He and his crew were to sail back to Jamaica where he owned a beautiful home by the seashore. The wealth of the world was his. Boldly, I began my testimony. He stopped

me, saying, "I'm a Jew. This has no real meaning to me." I
asked questions seeking to keep the conversation open. (A rule
of thumb, long since learned, is to ask a question when you
don't know what to do next in a witnessing situation.) Finally,
he loosened up and told me much of his life story. Winding
down he asked me, "What were you doing in Jamaica? Do you
work for the church? You telling me you don't get paid? Why?"
I proceeded with a widened version of my testimony. As we
circled to land in Miami, I urged him to at least read the New
Testament and make a decision for himself. He took me by the
hand to say good-bye and concluded, "I'll read it. You are very
happy and satisfied with life. I am very sad and lonely, even
with all my things."

Kingston Again

I returned to the beautiful island one additional time with
Billy Massey from Alabama to teach a lay evangelism school
at the Queen Street Baptist Church. We arrived at the church
on Saturday morning at 10 o'clock for our second teaching
session. Not one person showed up at the appointed hour.
Fifteen minutes later there still was no one. We began a two-
man prayer meeting; "Lord we know You brought us here.
We've come to do Your work, not ours. We are powerless
without You. If anything is to happen, You must move in our
midst." I heard the shuffle of a chair, then another, and another.
Within a few minutes the room was filled with people.

That afternoon thirty-five went out. Billy approached a man,
opened his Bible after asking a few questions, and read Scripture to him. As he was reading and talking, two men slowed to
listen and moved on. The man Billy was sharing with accepted
Christ. A few steps away one of the two asked, "Are you
missionaries?" "Yes," I answered. "Then tell us about Jesus,"

said the other. Billy opened his New Testament again and led both of them to Christ.

After preaching at Queen Street Church the next morning, I went to their small mission for the Sunday evening service. Because of the noise and confusion and children running back and forth, preaching seemed to be out of the question. Instead I gave some instructions and ask the folks to write their testimonies. I read a tract afterwards. As I neared the end of the booklet, a teenage girl began to weep. One of the ladies discovered she wanted to make a profession of faith. Dr. Horace Russell, pastor of the Queen Street Church, and his wife had been praying for the girl for many months. Her father was a government official. They hoped to reach the family through the daughter.

Before we left Dr. Russell shared with us the need of a dental chair and instruments. Each Saturday, professionals from Kingston, doctors, lawyers, dentists, and others, gave their time and talents to the needy without charge at the church. If the dental work was to succeed, the equipment had to be secured. Massey had a friend back home who worked for a dental-supply company. He asked him to help. The company donated the chair, and it was on its way a few months later.

5
Far Eastern Treasure

Look! I tell you, lift up your eyes and scan the fields, for they are already white for harvesting (John 4:35, Williams).

"You're from another land, a different culture. This won't work here. No one will let us read that tract. We can't do it." The huge Korean pastor interrupted me.

I had come to Korea with a layperson, Jerry Brannen, along with Max Cadenhead and Jim Ponder. We were part of a three-year partnership effort by Florida Baptists and the Korean Baptist Convention. Max and I were to conduct leadership witness schools in two cities and rejoin the other two in Seoul later. The day before we traveled down country from Seoul to Kwangju. It was harvest time. Figures were bent double in the fields, harvesting rice. The green rolling hills, dotted by small houses and villages, fell away to flatness. Most of the farmers were bent, not only in toil, but also in sin, worshiping dead gods—Buddhists, Confucionists, shamanists. Some worshiped spirits in trees and mountains, others depended on the flesh, or great thoughts and teachings of men long since dead and still in the grave.

After the interruption, I turned to Virgil Cooper, one of our missionaries, and asked, "What's happening?" He interpreted. Max spoke up, "Let me answer." Standing he said, "Go out this afternoon and try what we're asking you to do. Then let's talk again."

We stopped for lunch. My appetite was gone! Questions flooded my mind; "What if it doesn't work? What if this pastor is rebuked by someone on the street? A negative report would. . . . Then what?" We ate little, prayed much.

My visitation partners were Cooper and a young deacon. Another of the skeptical pastors followed. I handed my testimony, written in Korean, to a man on a bicycle. He stopped, read it, and told us he knew Jesus as Savior. As we walked, I kept praying, "God, You must do something or we're sunk." The deacon took us to a nearby office where a Christian friend worked as manager. He inquired if there might be someone to whom we could witness. We were ushered into a large conference room. In about ten minutes the manager returned with a man and woman.

Seven of us sat around an oval table as the two read my testimony. Cooper asked some questions, moved to a chair between them and shared the booklet, *Seven Steps to Peace with God* by Billy Graham. The skeptical pastor watched every move. We prayed. Both received Christ as Savior. I wanted to open the windows and shout, "Hey, world, it works! I mean He's real! It's true. See, Jesus saves. Right here, now!" Instead, I silently thanked the Lord as Virgil gave them some materials and shared beginning words of discipleship. As we prepared to leave, the young man said, "Earlier today I had a feeling this was to be a special day. It really is special. Thank you for coming so far to tell me what I needed." We stopped on the steps outside to offer thanks. This was a miracle!

As we finished praying the deacon spoke to a man coming down the steps. He returned the greeting and stopped. I stuck out my hand with the testimony. He read it. Amidst the roar of traffic and passing people, Virgil shared the tract. He also committed his life to Jesus! Virgil secured some information from him, we prayed again and turned to leave. "Wait," the man said. "I want to tell your friends something. Today I came to work sad and more lonely than ever before. My wife and I have had many problems. Yesterday she left and took our baby, to return no more. Just a few minutes ago I was released from my job. Everything was hopeless. I walked down these steps wondering if there is anything worth living for. Then I saw you praying. I thought, *Could there be?* Thank you for showing me there is. I can't thank you enough!" He wiped his eyes and walked away. After a few steps I said to Virgil, "You report first at the church."

Virgil rose to speak. The huge Korean pastor who had interrupted earlier in the day, began to make his way to the front. Virgil stepped aside. The pastor told of attempting to talk to three or four who would not listen. Excitedly, he added, "Two heard my testimony and listened to the booklet. Both received Christ, . . . I used the book. It works!"

What works? Not a booklet. Or a method. Or great words of persuasion. It is God Himself in our midst in the Person of the Holy Spirit, as we step out and speak His name even in precarious, uncharted territory. "The Lord hath done great things for us; whereof we are glad. He that goeth forth and weepth, bearing precious seed, shall doubtless come again with rejoicing, bringing his sheaves with him" (Ps. 126:3,6). In the Korean rice fields that day there was a bountiful harvest of thousands of acres. The Lord of the harvest was also bringing forth His harvest—human souls.

In June 1980 we returned with two-hundred to preach and witness in the five largest cities in Korea. Mickie and I spent our first week at Yoido Baptist Church, pastored by Han Ki Man. Five witnessing teams went out from the church daily for eight hours. Each team included a person from the United States, either myself, Mickie, one of two other ladies, or John Kellar, an Orlando pastor.

My wife's interpreter came from a wealthy family, as did a number of members of the Yoido church. She agreed to assist for two days. To our surprise the third day she was at the church when we arrived. Walking up to Mickie she said, "This is the Lord's work. It is most important. I am here."

The next day God moved as she expressed a burden to Mickie, "If my sister who lives miles away comes here, will you share with her?" The next day the sister answered *no* when asked if she had peace with God. She said to Mickie, "That's why I'm here." She received Jesus and stayed to make her profession public that night. Another young woman said to Mickie after her conversion, "It is God's will you have come. I have been searching for God. I studied trying to find Him. Now I know Him!" John Kellar spoke to a high-school assembly, and sixty-four students received Christ. Jim Ponder preached to 425 Korean troops. Most all of them responded to the invitation. He felt they were confused. Asking them to sit down, he restated the gospel and gave a second invitation. They rose again!

Korean Christians prayed before and after daybreak. Laypersons, musicians, and preachers witnessed door-to-door every day for many hours. Singing and preaching took place in the churches every night. The harvest continued. The great God, the Lord Jesus Christ alive in our midst, was performing miracle after miracle. "Day after day they regularly attended the temple; they practiced breaking their bread together in their homes, and eating their food with glad and simple hearts, constantly praising God and always having the favor of all the people. And every day the Lord continued to add to them the people who were being saved" (Acts 2:46-47, Williams). The Book of Acts came alive before my very eyes during those days.

Pastor Han Ki Man asked if I would speak to his men on Saturday morning. He sent a car to pick me up at 5 AM. His laypersons had been praying for over an hour when I arrived. As I waited, my own prayer went up, "Oh God, I have nothing to tell these men. They know You so much better than I. Help me Lord! Through the voices of these in a language I do not understand, You speak worlds to me."

Years later I was to hear Fred Wolfe, pastor of the Cottage Hill Baptist Church in Mobile, Alabama, say, "There is a call that is higher than the call to preach. It is the call to prayer. God puts a premium on prayer." Those are not idle words with Wolfe. He meets with his people three mornings a week to pray. Is it any wonder he pastors one of the strongest growing, ministering churches in the Southern Baptist Convention? He and his people pray and go.

The following week we moved to a small church on the edge of Seoul. Don Jones, another of our missionaries, went with us to preach and walk the byways. Our meeting place was a small room over a grocery store on a crowded, noisy street. Inside were a few straight chairs and wooden benches. The pastor had only one suit. He wore it each night. Far removed from Yoido, we were now to see some of the common folk of Korea. My partner was an English teacher. His wife cooked a Korean meal for us one evening, including the world-famous dish, *kimchi.*

As we prayed one rainy morning, he said, "Let's go." Driving along a muddy side street, he stopped at a lumberyard. I waited as he approached the manager. They moved toward a small enclosure and motioned for me to follow. We went in. This was the manager's home! His wife and child were inside. We sat on the floor in one of two small rooms in a circle as the wife served refreshments. That is the time-honored way you are confirmed as a guest by the Koreans. Our host's brother came in. We presented the gospel to all three. One after another, all three were saved. Before leaving we invited them to the evening service. The brother began to cry. His baby had died the day before and the burial would be that afternoon. Before leaving I prayed, thanking God for saving them and asking for comfort. They felt my heart, though they did not understand my words.

We witnessed to a great number of people the second week. Some accepted; others rejected. That's always true. I remember talking to an elderly Buddhist. He said when you die they put you in the ground and that's it. So much for Buddhism.

Two hundred went from Florida to join hundreds and hundreds of Koreans witnessing, preaching, praying, and singing. Over twenty thousand souls were saved!

We gathered our last morning in Seoul for reports and testimony before boarding our 747 for Seattle. Missionaries offered praise and thanksgiving for what God had done. Laymen were exploding as they went on and on about the miracles they had seen. Preachers and musicians joined in.

The twelve-hour flight back to the States was emotion filled for me; "God, I don't deserve to even see what You've done. My faith is so small beside that of these dear, dear people who truly love You."

Crossroads

I attended a meeting in 1979 with Jim Ponder in Dallas as Southern Baptists from across America gathered to consider a possible concept of personal witnessing. Jim was chairman of a task force appointed by Dr. Bill Hogue, then evangelism director for the Home Mission Board. The task force had the responsibility of developing alternative methods of personally sharing Jesus. The one presented had a multiplication factor as its centerpiece. It was to become known as Continuing Witness Training. Those in Dallas liked what they heard and urged full speed ahead. At that meeting I met Dr. Howard Ramsey who had recently joined the Home Mission Board as director of personal evangelism.

Ponder asked me to attend working sessions of the task force with him. I saw fourteen persons with varied witnessing backgrounds pray and labor over the direction of their work. They would break sentences, words, and paragraphs into pieces and discuss them. On one occasion we were to critique the work in small groups. I drew as my partner Dr. Roy Fish, evangelism professor at Southwestern Seminary. It was his work we were to critique! I remarked, "Dr. Fish, surely we're not going to do that." "To the contrary," he replied, "that's exactly what you and I will do." The layperson and the professor carefully considered his writings!

Ramsey came to Florida to preach in an evangelism conference. While there, he, Bob Allen, Dr. Stephen Olford, and I had lunch together. Afterward we joined in a prayer meeting in one of the hotel rooms. I listened as these men of God literally brought the Lord down into our presence! It was another of those mountaintop experiences that remains burned in my heart. While there, Dr. Ramsey talked to Mickie and me. He had attempted to find a Mission Service Corps couple to assist in the Personal Evangelism Department. None had surfaced. He challenged us, "God is leading me to you."

I was again stunned and began to argue with God, "Lord, You know I don't have all that seminary training, and I'm not equipped to do this, and surely Ramsey will find someone else, and that person will be just the right one. Right, God!"

We joined Ramsey and his work in October 1980.

I attended three Continuing Witness Training pilot seminars in Atlanta. Representatives from 120 churches across the Convention participated. They returned home and put the concept to work, sending evaluations to Ramsey and the task force during each step. Satisfied that God was truly in it, the task force completed its responsibility and left Ramsey the opportunity of introducing it into state conventions. After training me in two additional state CWT seminars, Ramsey assigned me a role as one of his national leaders. Our job was to assist the state evangelism director and local church members as they trained pastors, staff and lay leaders in the concept. They would return to their local church and implement the process. I began to travel to the four corners of America and into its heartland, over and over again.

All the while, the economic condition of the radio station in Augusta, Georgia continued to deteriorate. The notes I had guaranteed were appreciably beyond $600,000. God was doing so many miracles before my eyes that the economic problems paled.

6
Silver and Gold

Silver and gold have I none, but, such as I have give I thee (Acts 3:6).

Oregon

Tears trickled down his red, wrinkled face, settling into a rough, dark beard. Frail, with most of his teeth missing, David Carter moved toward the front of the small room in a frame building in inner-city Portland, Oregon. His light shirt and loose jacket were hardly enough for the cold outside. As he took Troy Smith's hand, the warmth in their faces pushed the cold and cruelty of the streets aside. David, just this side of a thirteen-year binge, was making his profession of faith in Christ public. After talking to Smith a few minutes, he turned to the twenty-five or so in the morning service. Pointing to two laypersons Carter said, "They told me about Jesus. And Jesus saved me yesterday. I've been in the hospital for two weeks with pneumonia. They found me on the street and took me there. They visited me every day. I've stumbled for a long time. But these men and Jesus are holding me up." Clint Sams and Dean Moxley had led Carter to Christ.

On the second row Roy Mimms leaned on his cane, his head cocked to one side. A days-old beard covered most of his tobacco-stained, weather-beaten face. He looked older than his fifty years. A few weeks earlier, Roy had given his hand to Pastor

Smith and his heart to Jesus. For fifteen years he had lived in a shantytown built underneath the elevated streets leading in and out of Portland. Now he was staying in the basement of Dean Moxley's home, out of the miserable, cold, wet weather. The next day Roy showed me a dog-eared copy of the February 1986 *People* magazine. There were words and pictures about him on three pages, the story of Portland's most famous down-and-outer.

Seated near Roy in the service were two blind people. One had tapped time with his fingers during the song service. Just down the row was a woman, hair disheveled, teeth missing. Others in the small congregation, neat and clean-cut, had responded to Troy Smith's message with amens and praises. Half of the group was down-and-out, the other, caring, loving, and ministering to these whom the world had passed by. I asked myself, *How many are out there like these? Who will pick them up, give them a piece of bread, a bed, and tell them about Jesus? Will anyone? Most of us live at arm's length, or much further, from suffering and poverty.*

A year earlier Smith had answered God's call to pick up a fallen ministry in inner-city Portland when he, as chairman of the local pastor's conference, could find no one to take it. He resigned his church and began with his wife and two children. He had discipled and equipped three laypersons. They were conducting three Bible studies and two worship services each week in high-rise apartments surrounding Baptist Revival Center. In addition, they were daily reaching down to someone on the street in need, showing them Jesus in word and deed.

Nine years earlier, Troy, then thirty years old, had been an electrical engineer in Angola, southern Africa. In his wife's words, he was a "bright, successful engineer." On an extended vacation, they decided to see Africa. As Troy told me the story that afternoon he said, "During periods of quiet and rest, while taking in the awesome beauty of Africa, God began to deal with me. I asked, *Where am I going? What am I doing? Is there a God? Am I doing anything lasting and worthwhile with my life?* God sharpened His probe and within days Troy accepted Christ as Savior. A few days later he responded to a call to preach. Returning to America, he attended William Carey College in Mississippi. After graduation he moved to the Northwest as pastor of a church near Portland where he served for five years. With enthusiasm he exclaimed to me, "I've never done anything in life I've enjoyed more than what I am doing right now."

Why would a man leave a high-paying job in a respected profession making lots of money and wind up in a street ministry? God knows Troy's every step. Secondly, joy can never be measured by what we have of the world's goods. Real joy comes from being in the palm of God's hand, in His will. That's where Troy, his wife, and a handful of laypersons are in Portland, Oregon.

Following our CWT seminar classroom time each day, we went onto the street to witness. As we left, Troy would remind us, "Remember when you talk to someone, this may be their only chance, ever, to hear about Jesus." His wife Jamie, a tall, beautiful lady, boldly took a team. I asked David Carter to go with my team. I wanted to get to know him. Astonished that I would ask, yet with joy he joined us. My other team member was Adrian Hall, evangelism director of the Northwest Baptist Convention. What a trio we made, a former foreign missionary now leading a great area in evangelism, a smelly street person, and a run-down, old layperson! David would walk up to a person, break the ice, turn to either Adrian or me and say, "My friend would like to tell you something." And off we'd go talking about Jesus. When asked to give his testimony, David would say, "I'd be dead if it weren't for Jesus. I was sick and dying and He raised me up. I was also going to hell and He saved me!" The impact was so great I never considered giving him pointers!

On our last afternoon in Portland, David and Roy took us to the shantytown where they had lived for years. Our teams found people in darkened shacks, in tents, some with nothing more than a sleeping bag, blanket, or piece of cardboard. Men and women came out of the shadows, wild-eyed and frightened, others bright of mind. It was difficult to keep any of them on one subject very long.

Two of our men, a Japanese preacher, Hiroaki Yokoi, and Glen Perry, a layperson from another Portland church, shared with a Mexican waiting for the next freight train south. Presently all three knelt and prayed as the Hispanic man was born into God's kingdom. Seven teams went out. One person was saved. Seeds were planted elsewhere.

I walked along the railroad tracks with David attempting to leave something with him he could use in witnessing. He had his testimony. It was great. Now there must be Scripture of some kind. That faint, soft Voice spoke up, "Teach him to use John 3:16. He can remember that." We walked and I talked. He repeated and repeated. I told him God would use him mightily as a witness.

The question of what the church, God's people, could do for indigents would not leave. Somewhere in the wee hours of the night my answer came—these must have hope. That was it! In fact, everyone must have hope or is miserable. David and Roy now had hope. They had Christian friends. And they had Jesus. This pastor, his wife, and a few laypersons had thrown themselves into a never-ending battle with the devil. Their tools for warfare were simple, yet profound. First, there's a faith that depends completely on Christ, complete trust in the Holy Spirit to empower and accomplish all in every situation. Second, a peace that passes all understanding because they know this is God's mission and His business they are about. Robert Coleman wrote in *The Master Plan of Evangelism,* "There can be no dilly-dallying around with the commands of Christ. We are engaged in a warfare, the issues of which are life and death, and every day that we are indifferent to our responsibilities is a day lost to the cause of Christ."

I told David, Roy, and the others good-bye. David had just received word he had a job as night clerk in a small hotel and would begin work the next evening. He stroked his face a couple of times, looked me in the eye, and said as I left, "It's gone. I shaved it off."

One Year Later

Clint had met a lovely young lady, fallen in love, and married her. A baby was on the way. His lay ministry now included witness to sailors. Glenn had left his high-paying job in the computer field and was leading a church in a small community near Portland, for what some would call "peanuts." Dean was equipping a former drug addict to witness. His powerful shoulders, arms, and handshake, coupled with a soft, loving spirit seemed to personify what Jesus would have a tough construction contractor to be. Then there was Roy. Beaming, calm he showed everyone handicraft that kept him busy. He had a small place of his own in a low-income rental area. I asked about David. He had left. No one had seen him in months.

Meet Susan, a pretty slip of a young lady in her twenties. She had been a ballet student, attended two colleges nearby. The devastating, gnawing specter of drugs had destroyed her dancing dreams. In the midst of the drug scene she knew she was far away from God. She was afraid to go to sleep at night for fear she would die and go to hell. Though she made a commitment to God years earlier, she was unsure of her salvation. One day she walked by the Baptist Revival Center, went in, and her life changed, again. Now she knew that she knew Jesus as

Savior. There had been no drugs for four months. Every minute of her spare time found Susan helping Troy, Clint, Dean, and Jamie reach out to the unfortunates. She cleaned restrooms, ran errands, and was helping a young man with terrible withdrawal symptoms. Her testimony and goals were simple, to love Jesus and become a Christian wife and mother.

"Troy, tell me, have you grown since I was here?" He replied, "Man we've baptized thirteen, seven others have joined, and now there are fifty of us. The monthly giving by this small group, many poverty-stricken but rich in the Lord, is fifteen-hundred dollars. Most of our people are tithers. They know how great Jesus really is!" God is providing all of Troy Smith's needs as he continues a ministry of love in one of America's lost cities! How silly of me to ask a man like Troy if he'd grown any! Better ask myself!

Colorado

I've skied through blinding snowstorms in Aspen, soaked in the golden sun of Capri and Majorca, watched bullfighters swirl, turn, and stalk in Spain, fished in ice-cold, pristine Canadian waters, studied matchless masters' works in the Louvre in Paris and the Prado in Madrid, watched stage productions in London and on Broadway, stood on the highest hillside in Grenada in the West Indies and looked toward a mighty, rushing ocean, cruised the Rhine, awed by the grandeur of castles, and wandered thru endless miles of the Rockies and Alps.

Yet all of this pales compared to the elation and joy of hearing a poor Indian sun worshiper lay aside his dead gods to proclaim Jesus Christ, King of kings and Lord of lords, Savior, the One and Only Living God.

Dusk settled as we made our last ski runs of the day at Snowmass, Colorado. It had been one of those days God had

designed in perfection beyond description. Light snow covered
the trails early in the day. The air was truly as pure as new-
driven snow. Boughs bent with their load. Winds were light and
the sunshine warmer than a cozy fire. Falls and spills were far
between. We were exhausted.

As we skied off the slope down a trail near our door, I noticed
Tony standing on the balcony of our condo unloading firewood.
His laced leggings barely kept out the snow and cold. Long,
jet-black hair, dark piercing eyes, and bronzed skin burned
through the evening air. I brushed the snow from my cap and
bumped my boots as we greeted each other. Eager to respond
to my questions, he told me he was an Indian. His grandmother
taught him to be a sun worshiper. He knew no other religion.
Two of his fellow workers, curious, stopped to listen, one a
student, the other a miner. The student, member of a cult and
eager to have an input, interrupted. Tony was interested. The
miner listened also. Careful not to start an argument, I moved
around the student's precepts and tried to present the gospel.
Darkness fell, the cold increased, and they left. Mickie and I
prayed for all three that evening.

We checked out at noon the next day following a morning
on the ski slopes. Seated near the window of a nearby restaurant, I gazed out as snowflakes drifted into the rising steam of
an outdoor swimming pool. Abruptly Tony appeared on his
way to the condos. Hurrying outside, I caught him. Picking up
where I left off the night before, this time with no interference,
I shared what Christ had done for me and quoted Scriptures.
Under conviction, trusting with an open heart, Tony bowed his
head, and there on the sidewalk, made his profession of faith.
I thanked God for giving me a second chance.

A few years earlier I would have passed Tony with nothing
more than a nod or fading word. "Tell someone about Jesus.
That's for seminary graduates, super Christians, preachers, not

me! I can't do that. Why I'm a layperson! And, really now, I don't want to be embarrassed."

That describes many folk in today's Christian church.

Recently Mickie went visiting with a lady from a local church. They entered a home where the wife was a Christian, the husband lost. The wife became defensive of the husband, even though he admitted being lost and was interested in hearing. Mickie very carefully presented the gospel, not wanting to make the wife angry. At the end the husband delayed, said he would wait. He was not ready. Outside, Mickie's partner said, "We were there too long. I was very uncomfortable. This really isn't for me." The devil loves such an attitude! If he can defeat us during a witness attempt, by making us uneasy or afraid, he's happy. As long as a person is truly interested in hearing about Jesus, I continue, all day, one hour, however long! Of course, we are to love others and not argue. We must remember however, that a level of discomfort comes when we talk to a lost person. Jewish and Roman leaders became so uncomfortable in Jesus' day that they crucified Him!

Years Later

Human blood smeared on five pentagram points stood as stark testimony to devil worship and the occult. Conflicting, desperate, and dangerous emotions poured from a teenager wrapped in all the trappings—rock T-shirt, earrings, and chains. The conversation moved to suicide. One page of his diary contained a prayer to Satan, ending with the statement, "If you're real, Satan, if you're there, Satan, help me!" Closing the diary, the young man told the three visiting from Circle Drive Baptist Church in Colorado Springs, Colorado, "I'm confused. I'm tired of living. I don't know if I can trust anyone. It'd be better if I ended it all!"

One of the visitors, a small Korean pastor, quiet for nearly an hour, asked in a hushed, soft-spoken voice, "Could I say something?" He looked at the teenager. "I grew up near Seoul, Korea, the first of ten children. We had no religion. I tried everything growing up. Later I entered law school. Don't ask me how many times I failed the bar exam. I lived like an animal. No goals, no purpose. Two businesses failed. I lost everything, no money, no willpower, no trust. My life was broken in a thousand pieces. I hated myself. I hated everybody. Finally in desperation I decided to jump off a mountainside and kill myself. I even failed at that! My sister urged me to read the Bible. I tried everything else. Why not this? I started on page 1 of Genesis. Soon it was clear I was a sinner. Also, God loves sinners. But in Genesis I could not find the way to God. Moving to the New Testament, a great revelation flashed through my mind. I knew God came into the world in the person of Jesus for me! In Mark 2:17, Jesus said, 'It is not the healthy who need a doctor, but the sick. I have not come to call the righteous, but sinners' (NIV). I gave everything over to Jesus. And he changed me. If you'll give everything to Him, He'll change you too! Would you?"

The teenager took the chains from his neck, removed the earring and pentagram, bowed his head as the four men held hands, and surrendered to Jesus as Lord of his life. There were tears of joy and prayers of thanksgiving! As the visitors prepared to leave the teenager asked for a ride to a nearby convenience store. He gathered all the paraphernalia, diary, and all, put it in a sack, and threw it in the refuse pile.

Abraham Lee, the Korean pastor, concluding his account of the visit as he spoke to the Wednesday night prayer meeting at Circle Drive Church, said, "While reading the young man's diary, I was reading my own. My heart was trembling and burning. I was crying. Then I opened my mouth."

During his earlier life in Korea, while continuing to study the Bible, Lee had received a call from God into the ministry as a pastor. It was in the twelfth chapter of Genesis. "The Lord had said to Abraham, 'Leave your country, your people and your father's household and go to the land I will show you' " (NIV, v.1). Lee had answered the call and had changed his name to Abraham.

God had once again brought together miraculous events and people to save one soul.

A brother was concerned and invited the teenager to church.

A Sunday School teacher heard a muted cry for help in the class he taught, and led a visitation team outside the church to present the gospel.

The church, led by Ed Tropp, discipled and equipped a Sunday School teacher to witness through CWT.

A Korean pastor traveled many, many miles from his homeland, a part of God's perfect plan to have him in just the right place at the precise hour. He gave his testimony.

My week in Colorado was one filled with honesty and confession. In the midst of our concentrated CWT training, one of the pastors, Mike, asked if he could say something to the entire group. "I'm frustrated. On the one hand I'm told there must be time for my family. Surely they're important. I'm told I must get daily exercise to protect my body. And then there are the study hours preparing for sermons. I must lead out in many, many areas of our church . . . visitation, counseling, praying, administrative duties. On and on it goes. And now you tell me I must be a model witness and equip others. I can't do all this!"

God chose Ed Gatlin, pastor of Calvary Baptist Church in Craig, Colorado, to respond. He had been called out of the Fort Worth, Texas, fire department into the ministry. After a year and a half at Southwestern Seminary, Ed moved to the town of fifteen thousand in northern Colorado to lead the congregation. During his seven years there the church grew from fifty, in Sunday School to three hundred. Hundreds had been baptized. All the way he role-modeled witnessing and equipped the laity to so do. In recent time the energy crunch had dealt a heavy blow to the town and the population dropped to seventy-five hundred.

Gatlin stood in silence, gathering his thoughts. "Our main reason for existing as pastors and churches is to reach the lost. Priority is critical. When we pastors place personal evangelism and soul-winning first, God places everything else in order. Our main problem as pastors is not lack of time, it's not lack of money, dedicated people, or other resources. Our main problem is we're not leading the lost to Christ, or, at the least, trying with all we've got to do so."

Gatlin went on to tell of baptizing ninety-three in 1986 as Craig was slowly evaporating. In 1987 he baptized just over twenty. He frowned, "I hate to admit it. The reason for the drop was me! I didn't go with my laypersons soul-winning. I made other visits. I didn't lead out. The equipping didn't continue. I have no choice. I must lead my people out to win the lost."

Russ Richardson, evangelism director of Colorado, told of his experience in the pastorate as he came to the end of his resources through busyness. Realizing he and his people were not reaching the lost as they should, he prayed for God's answer. He took a large note pad and divided it into two sections, the first a must-do list and the second an option list. Russ began to write as he prayed. When he finished he called his deacons together and explained the dilemma, "Men, I can't do all this and lead you out to reach the lost. What shall we do?" Richardson said the deacons took the responsibilities in the option list, did them and in turn supported him more strongly than ever. He concluded, "We tell jokes on deacons and laugh and criticize them. From that time on I have never made fun of deacons. We must have priorities. We must all work together as God's servants in the dying world around us!" Mike had his answer from two of God's special servants.

A few weeks after our seminar I received a bulletin from Scott Pool, pastor of Trinity Baptist Church in Gunnison,

Colorado. I quote: "On Sunday evening we had our worship service as usual. But what took place was anything but 'as usual.' The Lord used every aspect of our worship that night to encourage the many decisions that were made. He used the prayer time, the sharing, preaching, and singing. But it is this pastor's belief that the Lord especially used the testimony of Bob Hays. Most of you are aware he and I attended the CWT seminar in Colorado Springs. As you now know, it had a dramatic impact on our lives.

It was the sharing of Bob from his heart that really opened the door for the Holy Spirit to work in the many lives that evening. Bob confessed before the church his sin of omission, of not sharing his faith and really not being burdened for the lost. He made himself vulnerable. But there were no looks of condemnation, because we were all convicted along with Bob. He also shared the renewed commitment this had brought to his life, the new purpose that is now there to share his faith and to minister to those in need. What a glorious challenge he laid before us all.

We know that one seminar and one man are not going to cure all the problems of our community. However, with a fresh vision of our purpose and calling from God, Trinity Baptist Church can have a tremendous impact upon Gunnison.

New York

The day was blustery and cold, wintertime in Rome, New York. Twenty pastors and laymen were attending one of the first Continuing Witness Training seminars in the Northeast. During the third day of classes one of the pastors raised his hand and asked, "What are you folks planning after CWT? What happens when we get burnout from all these programs?" I delayed, knowing God's answer would be the right one but that mine, off the cuff, could be disruptive. That evening, seeing my frustration, Walt Tommy, a Washington, D. C. pastor, asked if he could answer the next morning. "Please do," I said, relieved.

The heart of his reply has stayed with me. He responded, "When we undertake as pastors to personally perform most of the ministry of the church, ourselves, the inevitable result is burnout. We *must* disciple and equip the laity and set as our goal the facilitation of a ministry, as God leads, for every member of the church. Burnout is misplaced priority. As pastors and leaders, we must choose, we must establish priorities in our own ministry and in our lives. If we don't, we'll always be frustrated."

My two visitation partners were pastors from Long Island. A black man with a bandage around the top of his head answered the first door. My first impression was to ask if we could return. But as soon as I told him we were from Grace Baptist Church, he stepped back, opened the door, and invited us in. He was eager to talk. There had been a minor accident at the air force base where he was stationed, but he was fine. I moved to spiritual matters and into the gospel. A short time later his wife came in the front door. She insisted we have refreshments. After visiting for another ten minutes, I started witnessing again, this time including her. About the time I quoted Romans 3:23, "For all have sinned, and fall short of the glory of God" (NIV), she yelled, "Stop." I did. Raising her voice, she said loudly, "This business about God is a fairy tale. I pray and it's just like vapor. Nothing happens." On and on she went. Sensing deep trouble, I looked to my two partners; one was searching Scriptures, the other praying. She finished. The Holy Spirit prompted my question, "Could one of my friends pray?" She gave him permission, he prayed, and I proceeded, "[Salvation is] Not of works, lest any man should boast" (Eph. 2:9).

Within a few minutes, she interrupted again. This time she turned to her husband and lashed into him with a verbal tirade.

"If you'd just do what you're supposed to do in this family and be the kind of husband you ought to be. . . . " On she went. Both of my partners were praying. She ran out of breath and I told her I'd finish in a few minutes if it was OK. She said yes and I completed the gospel with questions leading to a commitment. Remembering her hostility, I turned to the husband and looked to him for the answers. I waited. He looked straight down, head in hands. Silence. We prayed. Silence and more silence. By this time we had been there over an hour. I knelt on the floor between them and said, "I'll pray once more. If God leads you to make a commitment, please do so." As I looked up, tears were slipping down the cheeks of the husband. "I've done it. It's all settled," he said with a big sigh!

Turning to her I said, "I couldn't sleep tonight unless I ask you if you'd do the same thing." She refused. One of the pastors had a background similar to hers. He shared his testimony and quoted Scripture and we made ready to leave. She looked at me and ask a searching question, "How did you decide to come to our house?" I answered, "Someone at the church asked us to come." With a look of unbelieving gratitude she said, "Did they really?"

On the way to the church the pastors said they had never seen a battle more real between the Holy Spirit and Satan. They prayed from the time we arrived till we left.

I was ready to leave when we arrived. We were invited in. I was shaken by a tirade. God settled a heart. I was shaken again. God again quieted and settled the waters.

Only the Holy Spirit can accomplish the positive from the negative. The Holy Spirit controls, convicts, convinces and holds us high no matter what the circumstance. God Himself brings the harvest.

Of all the apostles, Paul is the last we would count as having knocking knees. Yet listen as he wrote to the Corinthians in his First Letter,

Now when I came to you, brothers, I did not come and tell you God's uncovered secret in rhetorical language or human philosophy, for I determined, while among you, to be unconscious of everything but Jesus Christ and Him as crucified. Yes, as for myself, it was in weakness and fear and great trembling that I came to you, and my language and the message I preached were not adorned with pleasing words of worldly wisdom, but they were attended with proof and power given by the Spirit, so that your faith might not be in men's wisdom, but in God's power (2:1-5, Williams).

New Mexico

Slowly swinging in the wind, the cable car crept up the mountainside. Far into the sky hang gliders drifted over a precipice. Hundreds of feet below jagged boulders waited. Ahead was Sandia Peak rising over ten thousand feet into the heavens. To the west a clean desert view of seventy-five miles was centered by Albuquerque. The last steep gorge suddenly dropped away, taking my breath. The wind whistled as I timidly looked over the side. Startled, I thought, *What would it be like falling, no hope, through a void, crashing! Lostness, separation from God, that's what it's like!*

I remembered the day before in Dallas. Hurrying to make my plane connection, I arrived to find my seat taken. A young lady with long, blond hair began to move, "We have your seat," she said. Out of breath, I motioned for her to stay. Within minutes we were airborne west. I settled back for a short nap before meal service.

"That was nice of you. Do you travel a lot?" the woman asked. "yes, about half the time," I replied, yawning. She introduced herself and her husband and told me they were returning from a vacation at a luxurious Mexican resort. They were going home to Colorado. "What do you do," she queried. I explained my Christian work, and asked about her religious background.

She was raised Catholic, her husband Lutheran. Both had been divorced and they now were Episcopalians. "Sounds like you got most of the bases covered" I chuckled.

Looking very serious, arching her eyebrows, she nearly whispered, "You're not going to tell me how to be saved, are you?" Forgetting the nap, I got serious, "Well, as a matter of fact I'd like to. Tell me, have you come to the place in life you know for sure you have eternal life and you'll go to heaven when you die?" Her husband squirmed and looked out the window. She thought carefully, "I'm not sure we can know about that." I quoted 1 John 5:13, "I have written this to you who believe in the person of the Son of God, so that you may know that you already have eternal life" (Williams).

She flooded me with questions as we talked; "Why do you keep saying Jesus instead of God? How do I know the Bible is true? What about Mormons?" And, as I moved near the end of the gospel, "What happens if I do this and then sin again?" She looked at her husband and said, "I've never in all my life talked to anyone like this about these things." I paused and posed the critical question, "Would you receive God's gift of eternal life right now?" She said yes. I led her in prayer and told her how to begin to grow as a new Christian. Because she had no New Testament, I gave her mine, one I had carried a long time. Her husband was satisfied as he was. One and a half hours had raced by.

God prepared her heart as many had planted and watered. I was allowed to see the harvest as the Holy Spirit convicted and brought her to commitment.

The devil fought. Food was served while I talked. I refused mine. She was dressed scantily. I kept my eyes on her face. I was tired. The Lord refreshed. Her questions puzzled. God gave answers.

Philippians 4:13 describes the witness' source of power. "I

can do anything through Him who gives me strength" (Williams).

The cable car eased to a stop. My host Chief Lawson stepped off. He had preached in a small mountain church that morning. Six had responded at invitation time. We rejoiced as we had lunch on the mountaintop, Sandia Peak.

A cool fifty-five degree breeze made us step briskly as we boarded the cable car for our return. Thousands of houses, ribbons of streets, and highways filled the scene below; 70 percent of the nearly half-million people in Albuquerque are lost.

The next morning I met Gerald Farley, church administrator and CWT director at Hoffmantown Baptist Church. His preparation for our seminar was thorough and meticulous. As a layman, he was busy reaching lost people and equipping others to do so.

Hoffmantown is no ordinary church. Norm Boshoff is no ordinary pastor. Born in South Africa, he received seminary training in America. This was the only church he had pastored. Later in the week he spoke to our pastors. "Evangelism is an absolute priority here. The Bible says go. Nowhere does it say come. Some in the church have the gift of evangelism. All must evangelize." Holding his right hand high he added, "The pastor of the church must fly the flag. He must lead the charge week by week!"

On Wednesday evenings at Hoffmantown a major visitation and witnessing effort takes place. After a meal together, Sunday School workers hold their class meetings, and up to three-hundred members spread out across Albuquerque witnessing and building bridges. A group of laymen conduct the prayer meeting. Boshoff goes out. He says if his people listen and respond to his two Sunday sermons, two per week are enough. At weekly staff meetings, everyone is asked to tell about their times of witnessing during the week.

On a return visit, I went with the adult education director,

Jim Tomberlin. Strong describes his witness. He presented the gospel twice that evening, once on a back porch and once in a home. There are a number of reasons this church has grown so dramatically. The overriding, primary one is that the church moves outside its four walls into the community. And when the members come face to face with others, they witness. Of course they invite folks to church and enroll them in Sunday School, but they present the gospel also. Failure to do so explains the lethargy most churches find themselves mired in. During the summer of 1986 fifty-four teams of witnesses went out each week during training at Hoffmantown. The next summer seventy-four teams were involved. Oh that the average church across America could catch the vision of Hoffmantown's leadership and laypeople!

Karl Heim in his book, *Christian Faith and Natural Science* wrote,

> The church is like a ship on whose deck festivities are still kept up and glorious music is heard, while deep below the waterline a leak has sprung and masses of water are pouring in, so that the vessel is settling hourly lower though the pumps are manned day and night.

It is not primarily size or money or great location that determines the direction of a church. The determination is made at the site of greatest worship, the highways and byways of life, every day.

During one of our nights at Hoffmantown, I was teamed with a geologist who had fallen on hard times because of the oil crunch. We had a lot in common! He had some witness training and wanted more. As we left he asked "Have you ever walked up to a perfect stranger and witnessed to him?" I told him I had. "That would floor me," he exclaimed. As happens on occasion, we found no one at home on our list of prospects. As we searched for a phone I saw a man picking up trash. We stopped and approached an Indian named Joe Pecos. In less than five minutes he admitted he didn't know he'd go to heaven if he died. He agreed to let me give him more information. With traffic whizzing by, he listened and then committed his life to Christ. Noting his address, we invited him to Bible study and church services and gave him a booklet, promising someone would visit him and his family. The geologist shook his head as we drove off.

During my return visit a year later, I went on a team with Micki Stricklin. She had just concluded her first cycle of continuing witness training. As we drove by a park on our way to an address, we saw four teenage girls sitting in a circle talking. We stopped and the girls let us share. Only one could speak English and it was halting. I decided to try to explain John 3:16 to them. One attempted to interpret for the others. I struggled. "For God so loved the world, . . ." and I labored over a simple explanation. It seemed our effort would be in vain. One of the girls pointed to a friend approaching. I questioned, "Can she speak English?" "Si [yes]," one replied. The fifth teenager joined us and in perfect English helped as we led her and the other four to Christ using John 3:16!

It is not our profoundness, or great skill, although all of us need to be trained to witness. God does honor preparation. Once we are trained God can use us more effectively. Yet we must never forget, it is the Lord who intercedes and supplies everything! Over and over again we see our weakness turned to strength by the Holy Spirit. We fail to even go, lest we depend entirely on God. The most difficult doorknob to turn on visitation night is the one on the door inside my house.

Virginia

Landing at the Richmond airport the next week, my plane hit the runway with a jolt, and bounced as the pilot added power and circled. He apologized, saying the tower had given him landing clearance, but once he touched down he saw an obstruction on the runway. This was already another exciting place!

On Sunday afternoon, one day before our CWT seminar began, I went visiting with Alice, an equipper in the local church. We were welcomed across the street from the church by a black man. Alice visited for a few minutes, then moved very easily into spiritual conversation. Step by step, without hitch or hesitation, she presented the good news. Her love for Christ and for people was transparent, up front, on her face, in her tone of voice, in every expression. The young father gave his life to Jesus. Alice could have said her health was not good, so she couldn't go. But she went. She could have said, "I'm afraid. I may be embarrassed so I'll not go." But she went. She could have said, "I'm too old for this and my memory fails me at times." She didn't. She went.

The newly appointed evangelism director from Oklahoma, Wayne Bristow, attended for certification with some twenty-five others. Dan Agee, Virginia's director, invited three additional pastors already in CWT to share with our group. They got probing, searching questions about the process. One wanted to know if CWT worked in small churches. He was answered by a pastor from the outskirts of Richmond in a small church, landlocked, no room to expand. His people had developed a maintenance attitude and were holding on. He told of going to a CWT seminar two years earlier. The year before not one person had been baptized! He returned home and began training his people as he went out with them. His words were, "We baptized ten people this past year. Keep praying for us. We haven't solved all our problems, but we're looking up instead of down!"

It seems I'm always looking for hard-to-find addresses on visitation. My two partners and I drove up to a large, two-story house sitting off the main road. A young woman in her twenties was sitting under a tree near the front. The layperson with us approached and opened conversation. She was nervous and distressed. Dark circles lined her eyes. Within just a few minutes a car drove up and a tough-looking man with no shoes or shirt got out. Pointing to him, the girl said, "That's my boyfriend." He approached, hair down to his shoulders. My first impulse was to let someone else on our team deal with him. Instead, I stuck my hand out, told him what we were doing, and asked if he'd join us. He sat down by the girl and said, "Get on with it." About five minutes later another car drove up. Again pointing to her boyfriend, she exclaimed, "He's not even supposed to be here. They don't allow him on this property!" My heart sunk knowing our opportunity was gone. Rising, I asked if they'd join us near the main road so we could continue. He agreed.

Getting in our car I told my partners we'd never see them again. To my surprise, when we approached the main highway, they were parked waiting for us. There, between the two cars, a few minutes later, they held hands and gave their lives to the Lord. We spent the next twenty minutes with immediate follow-up material and left for the church.

After returning to the church, we walked hoping we'd find someone to visit. A couple of blocks away, the staff member saw an elderly church member as she came outside. He moved across the street to talk. About the same time an elderly man came around the house and I crossed the street to visit with him. He told me his wife was the one who went to church. She "took care of those things."

I gave my testimony and inquired if he'd ever had an experience similar to that. "Nope, never have." Standing in the middle of the yard, he listened. His wife and my partner stopped talking and listened. He delayed when commitment time came. Placing my two hands on his shoulders, and looking straight at him, I pointed out that neither he nor I probably had very many years left on earth, maybe none! Surely this was so important he shouldn't delay.

With head bowed, in his yard, he asked for forgiveness and salvation. I said, "Go tell your wife what you've done." She already knew. They embraced and both wept. She told me she had prayed for him forty-six years. He was seventy-four. His name had been removed from the prospect list long ago!

Two Years Later

"You're not serious about going down there. Man that's tough, especially at night!" One of our visitation team leaders couldn't believe we'd go into the Westminister area. Go we did. Two were saved in the house my team visited. Everyone else had warm, exciting, and safe experiences.

Twenty-four Christian social ministry workers were involved in our witness training seminar in Virginia Beach, Virginia. A church planter said in conclusion, "We should have had this training before the first church was started. I've shared the gospel, but I never really knew how to draw the net." In three nights of visitation the net was drawn numerous times by twelve teams led by Pastor Ernie Roebuck and his folk from Calvary Baptist Church. Thirty-nine were saved.

Anna Keelin, for twenty years a CSM worker, was euphoric about the results. She said, "This has added a whole new dimension to my ministry. Proclamation has served to add balance to our social ministry."

I had known Dan Agee, evangelism director of Virginia, for five years. He was using many resources to equip and train pastors, staff, and laypersons to witness and reproduce themselves as equippers of witnesses in Virginia. Driving toward the Washington, D. C. area for another training session he expressed some profound truths.

1. Everything we do as Christians ought to lead the lost to Christ.
2. The church has developed a fortress mentality. We plan for our body, not nonchurch people.
3. Most of our leadership don't know how to witness and reproduce.
4. We react instead of acting.

Dan and I gave the cashier at our motel restaurant a tract and asked her to read it. The next morning as we paid our bill we asked if she had. She replied, "I read it yesterday afternoon, then again last night, and also this morning." Standing at the cash register, she received Jesus as Savior.

Five Miracles at Once!

Evidence of the great outdoors dominated; deer racks lined the room, a huge gun case filled one wall. Warm conversation about the latest deer stand fiasco and the one that got away brought laughter. Two hunters recalled adventure and comradeship.

Charles Corn of Hendersonville, North Carolina, led a team of visitors to an old friend's house on a cool fall evening. Charles had been a Christian for little more than a year. He was concerned about a fellow hunter. Before we arrived he told me, "I don't think he's ever been to church on a regular basis. But he'll talk to us." Three children sat following every word. After fifteen minutes I asked the father about his relationship to the Lord. He said everything was "OK." I asked if I could share with his son who was sitting near my chair. A teenager, he accepted Christ after hearing the gospel. Moving to a sister who sat nearby, I asked if she understood. A teenager also, she accepted Jesus as Savior. Turning back to the father who's testimony was somewhat unclear, I asked if he really wanted to settle the matter of his salvation and eternal destiny with his two children. His response was "Yes"! He bowed his head and prayed, giving his heart and life to the Lord.

By this time Charles and our other visitor, Nancy VunCannon, were on shouting grounds! Looking up from my prayer of thanksgiving, I noticed that the youngest son, near ten, had moved from across the room and now stood next to my chair. Sensing his deep interest in all that had happened, I asked, "Son, do you really know who Jesus is?" "Oh, yes, I went to Bible School once," he answered. After more questions and responses the ten-year-old prayed, expressing a deep desire to have Jesus as his Savior.

I was completely overwhelmed. No one could plan such an encounter. No one could know what to say under circumstances that brought four to the Lord! Only the Holy Spirit could cause this! Seven of us stood in a circle in the small, modest living room, holding hands, about to pray once more. From the hallway a lady in her thirties appeared and was introduced. I invited her to join our circle. Before praying I said, "Let's talk about your relationship to Jesus." Out of her trembling lips came these words, "I listened to every word you said. When my young son prayed to receive Christ, I did also."

Our visiting team had made an earlier visit that evening and was about to return to the church when Charles pushed me to make one more visit—this visit! How often we hurry past the lost on our way to the church house! How often, even when God lets us see the harvest, we leave more harvest in the field under our feet!

California

All the glowing, descriptive adjectives used to paint a mental picture of California are true. Roaring surf, mists creeping along rocky shorelines, crystal clear lakes in the upper reaches of towering, snowcapped mountains, palm trees, valleys filled with fruit trees and luscious vegetables—there's no end to the beauty and bounty provided by God. And there seems to be no end to the lost people. Monty McWhorter of the evangelism department says that 81 percent of the people in that state are lost. The population of the greater, Los Angeles metropolitan area varies, depending on who you talk with. Take your pick, ten million to fourteen million.

Mark Jappe, pastor of the Bryant Street Baptist Church in Yucaipa, met me at Los Angeles International Airport. Driving the eighty miles to the valley, Mark shared about his church and what was happening. He told me it was just as exciting to witness as to preach. Did I hear him right? I did. He had moved through two CWT cycles and was now ready to launch out in earnest to reach the lost.

Six teams knocked on doors Monday evening. One twelve-year-old boy was saved. Tuesday evening no one came to Christ. McWhorter and I prayed for more souls for the kingdom during Wednesday's outreach.

Denice is a single parent rearing three children in a modest home adjacent to the church. Twenty-year-old Stacey Manley sat in the living room sharing with Michelle, Denice's twelve-year-old daughter. Brother Jappe went to the kitchen to share with Denice. I prayed.

Fourteen-year-old Rob swept past me twice with hardly a word. I heard him on the carport working with an electric sander. I stepped outside. Trying to talk to him over the noise was difficult. The sander broke! Still kneeling, he listened. He received Christ. As I finished sharing the booklet "Welcome to God's Family," Michelle and Stacey came outside bubbling with the news of Michelle's salvation experience. Denice and the pastor joined us and told of Denice's accepting Jesus also! The mother said, "We've just prayed, Rob, that you'll make your commitment soon." The three of them embraced as they learned each had received Christ. Michelle exclaimed, "If my sister, who is three, were old enough, we'd wake her and finish the whole family!"

The bounty of the farmer's fields in California is great. The harvest of souls God has prepared in California is also great. The shortage is laborers for the fields. In his book *Every Member Evangelism,* Roy Fish quoted a great song leader, the late Charles M. Alexander "Anybody who is not doing personal work has sin in his life. I don't care who you are—preacher, teacher, mother, father—if you are not leading definite people to a definite Savior at a definite time, or trying hard to do so, you have sin in your life. If this is true, and it is, for disobedience to the Great Commission is sin—what a weight of guilt is resting on a multitude of Christians in the church today." I remember hearing leaders who obviously were not witnessing say, "Don't lay that guilt trip on me about witnessing." Fish is saying if we have a guilt trip about lack of witness, it is the guilt of sin. God is speaking to us. The way to clear all out is to begin right now, where we are and tell others about Christ.

Michigan

Snow was falling out of a gray, dreary sky as it had all day. In the warmth of a small apartment in Jackson, Michigan, Sam Howard was praying for a dear friend as I shared. Sam had talked to Earl many times about Christ. Always the answer had been the same, "Not now; later." Sam kept coming back.

We had arrived an hour earlier. Earl was short, balding, and stocky with a warm smile and big voice. On the wall were three massive deer racks. He recounted story after story of tramping in the Michigan woods through cold, biting winters and the bright sunshine of other seasons. In the midst of God's great creation he had found some simple satisfactions. But he did not know God. Earl was lonely and bitter having lost his job months before. As smoke curled from his cigarette, strong language slipped out from time to time; "I worked in a tough, tough place for many years. That's the way we talked. It was a way of life. Why, if I went to church, I'd probably say something bad and people would smell this cigarette smoke. They don't want me down there."

Sam stepped in, "God can help you clean up whatever needs cleaning up in your life, Earl. You can't do it alone. Like Bo said earlier, one of these days the consequences are going to be terrible unless you receive Jesus." How perfect are the words of witness God plants in our heart! I asked Sam to pray again for his friend. Through the tears of all three, Earl turned everything over to Christ, his tough language, the tobacco, his loneliness, and lost soul.

As we walked through the snow to the car, Sam continued to weep, "I asked God to save him many, many times. Now He has." Inside the car he shouted and clapped his hands. Sam was sixty-five years old with silvery hair, a man of many interests. He was retiring after thirty years with a large automobile manufacturer. He loved the outdoors. Rebuilding damaged airplanes was his hobby. His pastor, Milton Wood, said, "It's men like Sam who make being a pastor a joy. He's always there no matter when or where I need him."

On the second day of our seminar at Gorham Baptist Church, Sam and I visited the wife of a church member. She had refused to accept Christ on earlier visits. Before we left someone said, "I don't know what you'll find. You may not get very far." Sam had been there before. He was not too enthusiastic.

Maria answered the door and called to her husband, "Folks from your church are here." She joined us in the living room. In storybook fashion we presented the gospel and Maria became a Christian. God had dealt with earlier objections. She was ready.

On my final evening with Sam we were to see another miracle. (I believe it is a miracle every time God saves someone.) We drove into the countryside in bitter winter cold to find a seventy-four-year-old Sunday School member and her two sons, single and in their forties. Dirty dishes were everywhere. Clothes, boots, and papers were scattered about. It was a well-lived in house. Before long she and Sam were in conversation about one of her neighbors. She praised them, "I can tell you one thing about them. They don't just talk about being Christian. They live it. Really." She rode to Bible study with them. We led her to Christ.

I wondered if Sam would be able to drive back to the church. He danced, he prayed, he thanked God, and cried more tears of joy. "Bo, let me tell you what I've decided. I'm going to more than tithe everything to the Lord, my money, my time, everything. And I'm going to learn how to present the gospel. I am, I am!"

I saw the results of caring, loving Christians reaching out to the lost. Our lives are a series of relationships. We build bridges to others each day or we tear them down. Always we must speak about Jesus for He is the Good News.

Northern Woods

Tears came in torrents. With voiced trembling he sobbed out a searing story of three marriages, three families, children scattered, his heart now broken, "I'm such a failure I can't even visit my own children. It's been hard for me to try to talk to anyone about this. Will you pray for me?" Jimmie Jones, evangelism director for Michigan, asked those who would gather around to pray. Hands reached out. Another man began to weep. Across the room a young man stood up with tears flowing, "My father is an alcoholic. I'm afraid he's going to die. Pray for him." Another stood, "I've not been a witness. It's been all sham, this witnessing. I need God's help." On and on, hearts and souls opened in honesty and confession with petition and praise.

One hundred Baptist men had gathered two days earlier at Bambi, a snow-blanketed retreat in the heart of Michigan's great northern woods. After six hours of witness training we scattered across the countryside into homes and onto the frozen surface of Lake Houghton to practice what we had learned. On the lake and along the streets was a circus. A giant merry-go-round cut through the cold afternoon sky next to a beer tent at the lake's edge. Sideshow hawkers beckoned. Snowmobiles, three-and four-wheelers, cars, and trucks scooted across the frozen surface. Small shacks dotted the ice. Holes were drilled and flags flew as far as one could see. A fish-weighing station was filled with pike, sunfish, and trout. Nearby, amid the roar and confusion, the sides of a warming tent erected by the local Baptist association flapped in the stiff, freezing wind. Some of our hundred were moving in and out speaking to those who would listen. I approached a young couple sitting quietly near the back. Within minutes they were praying and making their commitments to Christ, another Divine appointment. Another occurred in a home nearby as a mother, father, and all five children received Jesus as Savior!

One day later on a Sunday morning, removed from the rushing world, we were preparing to leave for home. God decided to get us on His schedule. After music and testimony Jones and I were to give testimony and preach. But, before Jones could begin, the weeping and confessions began. As true revival happened Jones said, "I know when to preach and when not to. Now I won't preach." For over two hours confession, cleansing, petition, and praise continued.

As Jimmie and I drove to the Detroit airport we agreed we had seen and felt the hand of God move across our souls that morning! And it was more than I can describe.

The incredible beauty of Canada fills one's soul. The wilderness and mountains, the plains, rivers, the stark grandeur of the far northern country overwhelms. So does the vast number of lost people.

The first of two CWT seminars took place in Regina, Saskatchewan, in February. Temperatures plummeted to forty degrees below zero! Equippers drove over snow-packed, icy roads from Winnipeg and Saskatoon to assist. God convicted me about missed worship services and outreach assignments back home because of feeble excuses.

The next week I flew to Calgary and Willow Park Baptist Church. Pastor Charles Koenig demonstrated life-style evangelism vividly one morning. A young lady delivered a typewriter to his office. Instead of hurrying back to tell us *how* to witness, he spent time visiting with the lady, presented the gospel, and led her to Christ. She shared her Christian testimony for the first time with our group!

At lunch I asked a waitress, "Who is Jesus?" She hesitated, thought for a moment, and said, "I don't know." (We think everyone knows about Jesus; not so.) With only a few customers in the restaurant I was able to share brief words of testimony and leave a tract.

My visitation partners that week were James Stephens, a Saint Paul, Minnesota, pastor, and Shirley, a member of Willow Park. We were welcomed by a couple from Austria who had lived in Calgary four years. At the outset, the wife unloaded pent-up frustrations. She had no friends, and was very lonely. Her husband's family rejected her. Her father ordered her to go to church as a youngster, yet never went himself. She chain smoked as she talked. (Most times we'll never be able to present the gospel if we don't listen.) The husband, who spoke four languages, sat on the floor.

After we'd been there the better part of an hour, I asked if Shirley could share something really important with them. The husband used his French language New Testament to follow some of the Scripture passages. He asked questions, but said he was too bad to be accepted by God. The wife didn't believe God really loved her. After clarification, I asked Shirley to share her testimony. She told of a divorce, being an alcoholic, battered by problems with no hope. Her daughter had tried to witness to her many times. Near suicide one evening, she called the daughter for help. This time she received Christ. Her concluding words were, "I haven't touched a drop of whiskey since that night. God cleaned up my life. He saved me from alcohol and certain death, physically and spiritually." The barriers around both hearts were broken with the testimony. We knelt together in a circle as both confessed Jesus as Savior. There was a warm, warm celebration on a cold, cold night!

Most of us may not have a testimony as dramatic as Shirley's or the apostle Paul. Yet, in a powerful way the Holy Spirit can use words that tell about our Christian conversion and walk. If you've not already done so, pause right now and write your testimony in two hundred words or less.

Don't use churchy words or sentences—"washed in the blood," "filled with the Spirit," "walked down the aisle"—non-Christians won't understand their meaning. You should be able to recite it in two minutes or less. This is a guideline to four points you'll want to explain.

1. Here's how my life was before I received Christ.
2. God let me know I needed Jesus as Savior.
3. Here's how I committed my life to Him.
4. God has done so much for me since then.

After writing and memorizing your testimony, use it! The first step is to seek permission by asking a question similar to this, "Friend, I've never been able to talk about Jesus, but now

I can. Would you let me share what He's done for me?" Or, "I'd like to tell you about a really important thing that's happened to me." Then give your testimony. At the end ask if they've experienced anything similar to that. If you don't receive clear testimony of salvation, present the gospel, using a marked New Testament, "The Eternal Life" tract or John 3:16. "For God loved the world so much that He gave His Only Son, so that anyone who trusts in Him may never perish but have eternal life" (Williams).

You can explain John 3:16 in four parts. (Notice a verse of Scripture with each segment to assist in explaining. My personal comments are in parentheses. Scripture is in quotation marks.)

1. "For God loved the world so much." (He loves you and me and every human being.) John 10:10: Jesus said, "I have come for people to have life and have it till it overflows."
2. "He gave His Only Son." (For forgiveness of sin, wrongdoing, and that we could know God.) Romans 5:8: "But God proves His love for us by the fact Christ died for us while we were still sinners."
3. "That anyone who trusts in Him." (We must completely trust Jesus to be who He says He is and to do what He says He will do for us.) Ephesians 2:8: "For it is by His unmerited favor through faith that you have been saved; it is not by anything that you have done, it is the gift of God."
4. "May never perish but have eternal life." (From the day of salvation, we are in God's kingdom and one day will spend eternity with Christ in heaven.) John 14:3: "And if I go and make it ready for you, I will come back and take you to be face to face with me, so that you may always be right where I am."

Then there must be a commitment. It is not enough to have information about Jesus. We must act on it. We must turn all, our complete being over to Jesus. Romans 10:9-10 "For if with your lips you acknowledge the fact that Jesus is Lord, and in your hearts you believe that God raised Him from the dead, you will be saved. For in their hearts people exercise the faith that leads to right standing, and with their lips they make the acknowledgement which means salvation" (Williams).

Could it be that as you have read through these pages of testimony, you are not sure you are saved, or you know you're lost? Would you, with a simple prayer, turn all over to Christ? Right now? Pray this prayer, remembering it is the desire of your heart and your sincerity that matters to God, not simply the words.

"Lord I am a sinner. I believe You died for me. Forgive my sins. I trust You and give my life to You. Please be my Savior. Thank You for saving me."

Now go tell someone!

I have demonstrated how we can use our testimony and a verse of Scripture to lead a lost person to Christ. Let me hasten to add, however, it is best to receive personal witness training using one of several proven methods. The Baptist Sunday School Board has a number of excellent Training Center Modules available including "How to Witness" and "Training Sunday School Workers to Witness." The personal evangelism section of the Southern Baptist Home Mission Board provides state evangelism directors and churches with materials and support in teaching Continuing Witness Training seminars, (Lay Evangelism Schools), TELL, and Relational Evangelism. If we are taught by someone whose life-style is witnessing, we are more likely to "catch it." The pastor's participation and leadership in the local church is absolutely essential, no matter what method is used! Other laypersons and staff may assist. But, as Norm Boshoff of Hoffmantown Baptist Church in Albuquerque says, "The pastor must fly the flag!"

7
Diamonds in the Rough

The Son of Man has come to seek and to save the people that are lost (Luke 19:10, Williams).

Ernie

Softness of voice, an unassuming attitude plus a "country-boy drawl" and an humble spirit pushed a scarred and devil-dominated past into oblivion. When I first met Ernie Simmons in 1987, I felt sure he had been a Christian for many years. Listening to his testimony two years later I was overwhelmed. He had grown up on the wrong side of the tracks in Pinellas Park, Florida and was considered "poor white trash." Neighborhood children could not play with him. Prospects for anything beyond a poor, drab future were dim.

Riveted to my chair in a motel room in Oklahoma City on a cold, snowy day, I listened to the spinning story of this gentle man's past. The sordidness of earlier days stood as a monument to the forces of evil rampant in today's society. The present man stood as a greater monument to the power of Jesus to change any life!

Many years earlier through adversity, difficulty, and sheer determination, Ernie had become a highly successful Lockheed Aircraft executive in Atlanta. His future looked unlimited! All that he touched seemed to move him ever higher up the corporate ladder. One day an encounter with a simple man who could not read changed the direction of his life. Ernie met the owner of a salvage business and laughed because of the man's unlearned ways. As he saw what this man had done in accumulating wealth and the trappings of happiness, Ernie's laughter vanished. He said to himself, *I'm a lot sharper than this guy. Yet he makes over a half million dollars a year in bad years! That's for me! His wife and fellow employees were shocked that he would even consider throwing away a highly promising career with a major defense contractor.*

Ernie bought a cornfield and started his new business in Dallas, Georgia, January 1, 1968. Though he was not a Christian, because of his wife Edith's faith, he decided to tithe all that he made to the church to pacify her. The first year in business his net income was eighty thousand dollars. The following year he had to hire a CPA to care care of the money, now flowing in like the tide. His salary was a thousand dollars a day! His year-end bonus was fifty thousand. Ernie became so busy he carried on two telephone conversations at the same time, a phone in each ear.

The devil was busy carving Ernie Simmons into the kind of man he wanted. As he sat across the table, occasionally wiping away tears, his testimony continued: "I was called 'lying' Ernie. I'd tell anybody anything to make money. I constantly manipulated people. Whiskey was stacked in cases in my office. To those who could do me favors it was take what you want! There was a houseboat, two motor homes, an airplane, two Rolls Royces . . . all available to my 'helpers'. Free to those 'on the take' were tickets to baseball and football games. I bought real estate like mad and ultimately became the largest commercial landowner in Paulding County, Georgia. One young man on my payroll did nothing but buy property. Only two large companies paid more land taxes than I. I started a cable television company, bought a radio station, opened a motorcycle shop and an automobile-repair business. But the salvage business remained my road to great riches!

To give you an example of how low I had fallen, I bought 175 generators at public auction for only fifty-five dollars each. They were each worth hundreds of dollars. I knew who to see and the kind of preparation to make before an auction started. I always had an angle and I played everyone. There were surplus boats, airplanes, trucks, all easy to acquire using the right bait. The dollars rolled into my pockets in ever-greater amounts. My tithe checks were four- to five-thousand dollars a week, that's right, each week!" Ernie pushed his chair back and stopped.

Regaining his composure he continued, "I got angry at the church receiving my tithe. In a fit of frenzy I told my wife, 'No more tithe, no more money to that church. And another thing, you stop going to church. That's enough of that.' Looking back, Edith, my wife, has to be the greatest person in all the world. Everything she did pointed to Christ amidst all the sordidness of my life. Of course I whitewashed everything. She turned to me with a gentle, warm smile and said after my rash statement, 'I won't go to church if you tell me not to. But, you will have to answer to God for it!' I roared out of the house in a fit of rage. For hours I fumed and ranted and raved, alone. I returned to the house and growled, 'Forget it. Go on to church.' "

"By now my financial statement showed a net worth of $16.5 million. My personal bank account contained over a million dollars. The tithe stopped. The erosion began immediately. Every place I turned money started going out instead of coming in. Business deals went sour. Step-by-step, the world began to crash around me. My so-called friends turned the other way. I began to cave in. Within a short time I was frantically trying to figure out a way to protect and keep something. As I sat in my office one day, a mental wreck, Edith eased up behind my chair and whispered, 'If you don't start tithing again you're

going to lose it all.' Thoughts began to race through my mind.
. . . *Maybe God is real after all!* Willing to do anything to stop
the torrent of losses, I told her to start the tithe again. She did.
Immediately business stabilized. Losses stopped. I never again
made money fast. But business was steady."

God was preparing Ernie to listen to Him! He attended
church with Edith from time to time. One day he became ill and
took to his bed. No longer able to go on, he collapsed. God was
to use Edith to change Ernie forever. She went in and out of
his room, one of ten bedrooms in the house. Ernie said, "She
really loved me, the mean devil that I was. That in itself is a
miracle. I thought she was busy with housework. Instead she
was calling every person she knew. She asked them to pray for
me.

"Hours later as late evening approached she said, 'I know
what's wrong with you. You're under conviction!' I began to
pray. Nothing happened. I didn't want to discuss lying, cheat-
ing, and stealing with God. Edith asked me to kneel by the bed
with her. Like a flowing river God began to wash away all my
reservations . . . now I was willing to do anything God wanted.
I asked for forgiveness. There was true repentance. No longer
did I want to be a crook . . . a swearing, detestable human being.
'Oh God, whatever You want of me, I'm ready. If You want
me never to go back to that junkyard, that's OK. Lord, Jesus,
I want to be truly forgiven and a child of Yours.' " On September 4, 1985, God did a work of true salvation in Ernie Simmons's life!

"The preacher and my son came into the room. In the den
many of my wife's fellow Christians had been praying. It was
now ten o'clock at night. As the preacher shared with me he
asked when I'd like to be baptized. 'What's wrong with right
now?' I replied. Astonished, he and my wife began to call
church members and ask if they'd come to the church where
we were to have a baptismal service way into the night. And

come they did to see the county's biggest crook tell the world he was choosing Jesus! Near midnight in a church that would hold 250 folks, 235 sat in the pews. "All of my children and grandchildren looked different. The world looked different. I saw my dear, dear wife as she really was. As I came out of the baptismal waters the Glory of Jesus appeared! Oh, the word of God is so true. As Paul says in 2 Corinthians 5:17, 'Therefore if any one is in Christ, he is a new creation; the old has gone; the new has come.' "

Here again was living proof of God's great love for sinners. How marvelous and miraculous is the love of our Savior, Jesus! No matter how low we've sunk, no matter what depth of our sin, He stands ready with open nail-scarred hands to receive us in true forgiveness if we'll turn to Him in true repentance. That untold millions who are lost could know and receive this Truth, the greatest Truth of all the ages!

Ernie has given all over to our Lord. Truly, old things have passed away. He is busy starting churches near the great metropolitan area of Atlanta. In nine months, in the face of severe opposition, a work started from absolute scratch, in a building on a junkyard, over seventy-five had been baptized. One-hundred sixty-five attend worship services. A preacher has been called, a deposit on thirty acres of land two miles away has been made and plans are underway to build a house of worship for this new fellowship. As soon as the move occurs, Ernie says, under God's leadership he'll start another church in the same place. I asked, "Ernie there are churches all around your area. Why start more?" His reply, "I tried to find one that wanted to witness and train soul-winners and reach lost people and couldn't. So I figured God wanted churches started to do that."

Johnny Hunt, one of God's great servants and preachers has become Ernie's friend and helper. First Baptist in Woodstock, Georgia, where Hunt is pastor, supports Ernie's efforts. And Johnny has become a defender of 'God's new creation'. In

Johnny's words, "Man, there's a lot of things I did before God saved me that I don't want to talk about. Let's never condemn a man for what he was. Let's love him for what he is in Jesus Christ and be his true brother."

Rushing to catch my plane in the airport in Oklahoma City, I left Ernie busy telling a lady about Jesus. As I look at the walk of Ernie Simmons in this terrible world of sin, His footprints now resemble so closely those of Our Savior Himself!

Jerry

Opportunities for reaching people in our circle of influence is truly great. A Christian businessman in Milwaukee, Wisconsin, saw an open door during a time of recreation, walked through it, and released a chain of miraculous events.

I met Jerry Harden at Calvary Baptist Church in Clearwater, Florida, where he served as an equipper. He gave this testimony in our seminar.

"In early October, 1983, I sat alone in my bachelor apartment in Milwaukee. I was fifty-one, divorced, rich, powerful, and had a deep sense of guilt and shame. My wife and I had been apart for seven years. I was living 'the good life.' A year or so before a Billy Graham Crusade had came to Milwaukee. My wife attended and went forward. Before our divorce we had attended church 'for the kids.' I felt Christianity was for intellectual weaklings who couldn't control their own lives. My wife's decision in the crusade was OK. I was sure she needed to be changed, not me.

"The overpowering sense of shame and guilt I felt, got worse even under a psychiatrist. I played racquetball with a Christian friend. I couldn't understand how he could be a Christian and a businessman also. One day I asked him. After trouncing me soundly in our game, he told me. He led me to Christ! I was overwhelmed—to be forgiven—wow! What a miracle! My friend said the first people I should tell about my conversion was my ex-wife and children. Reluctantly, I agreed. They were surprised.

"Negotiations to purchase a small business in Florida were successful and I moved to Clearwater. I attended many churches, searching for Christian fellowship. Thanks to a good job of follow up by my friend back in Milwaukee, I was deeply into Scripture study. One day I came home to find a copy of John's Gospel, left by a visitor from Calvary Baptist Church. Next Sunday found me there. I went forward and publicly declared my newfound faith. Brothers and sisters in Christ visited me. I enrolled in Sunday School.

"My pastor, Bill Anderson, enrolled me in Continuing Witness Training. He assigned me to an older lady, Maxine, as my equipper. Not only did she help me with CWT, she took an interest in my family. She discovered God had placed a desire in my heart to have our family reunited. She prayed and encouraged me and shared my need with fellow church members. In the meantime I learned, not only how to share my faith in Christ, but also sound Scriptural doctrine which cleared up questions in my mind.

"My ex-wife and children came to visit and see for themselves if I really was a new creation in Christ. Then in July of 1984 we were remarried. Subsequently, my daughter was born again and we all began our new life as a Christian family!

"Isn't that just like our God! He takes a worthless sinner, firmly planted on the garbage dump of life, and through the loving witness of caring Christian friends brings about a new birth. Then He reunites a family. And gives us purpose for living and finally lets us tell others about it!

"It is awful to be apart from God. The emptiness, the slavery of sin, the burden of a purposeless life piles up, and the load gets heavier each day. What a joy it is to be a Christian and to be equipped to to tell others about Christ."

Jerry finished his testimony. The impact remained.

What if the businessman had not been sensitive?
What if he had not presented the gospel?
What if he had not pointed Jerry to God's Word?
What if the church had not sent visitors to Jerry?
What if Sunday School members had not followed up?
What if Maxine had not cared?
What if Calvary's pastor, Bill Anderson, had not decided long ago to equip his people to witness and minister beyond the walls of the church?

A chain of events started during a racquetball game. Only in eternity will we know where they lead.

Gene

Rugged and bronzed, he is a take-charge guy. His family calls him "Chief." Lines etched by life's concerns are carved into his face. As Gene York rises to speak of Jesus' love, his big heart melts. Listen with me.

"About twenty-five years ago my wife, our three sons, and I attended a church south of town almost every week. We were not Christians but we wanted to go. One Sunday morning a squabble developed right in the sanctuary. We stayed for that service but never went back. We were turned off church for many years.

"Through the years I felt I needed no one. I thought I could do my own thing. I didn't drink, smoke, run around, and took care of my family, and I felt was a decent person. Then came a time when I no longer had control over things. The tragedy of losing my youngest son was the worst. There was no coping. Something had to change and I couldn't do it on my own.

"One day while at the cemetery where my son and father were buried, I knew what I had to do. I asked the Lord to help me, to take control of my life. He answered my prayer. My life is so different now. I've found the answer to many of my problems and have a different outlook. I have a desire to help others become Christian and to help them become stronger, more faithful, and dedicated to our Lord. Since I was saved three years ago, my wife has been saved; also my two sons-in-law, the wife of my dead son, two grandsons, an older brother, and the parents of my daughter-in-law. As you can see, I am fully blessed. It may seem I'm praising myself, but all the glory is for God, for without Him I can do nothing."

During the first three years of his Christian walk, Gene completed the *Survival Kit 1,* certified as a witness in the CWT process, became an equipper and trained two others to witness, attended a prayer seminar, worked through MasterLife, and served as a facilitator. When I was at University Baptist Church in Middletown, Ohio, where he is a member, Gene was attending Sunday School and an additional Bible study. His pastor, Nolan Phillips, told me, "On the surface I didn't see the possibilities when he was saved. But he proved to be a diamond in the rough." Phillips wrote me later, "Gene York has led another to the Lord in CWT and a second young man he met has asked him to come and pray with him to receive Christ. He has a growing zeal for souls that's great to watch."

Nolan Phillips celebrated his seventeenth anniversary as pastor of the church the Sunday I was there. A slow building process had been going on for years. The pace has now accelerated. He gives much of the credit for the increase in attendance and baptisms to Continuing Witness Training. In 1986 they baptized fifty-eight. The year before it was twenty-two. He says, "I thank the Lord for the difference. I believe we would have had a decline as the church grew in size since most of the earlier baptisms were pastor related and now many are a result of lay witnessing." University is not a large church in size. About 225 attend Sunday School. It is in pioneer country, not in the Bible Belt. Nolan has firmly committed his ministry at University Baptist Church with his people and is leading them onward as he preaches, equips, and disciples.

Want to know how to grow a church? Ask Nolan.

Want to know about the joy of witnessing? Ask Gene.

Jack Stanton, former vice-president of the Southern Baptist Convention and a leader in lay evangelism for many years, said in a recent conference, "We're going to have to give an account of how we spend our energy and what we've talked about. It takes times, talent, and tears to reach people. People cry over soap operas on television. We need to see lost people as if they had cancer. We hurt for blind, crippled people, but not for lost people. Our prayer meetings are more for sick bodies than sinful souls. If you want something up there, you must send something ahead."

Bo (a Young Lady)

The sparkle in her eyes tells of consuming joy. There was no way to tell that just a few years ago she had been a church dropout. This preacher's daughter told our Atlanta seminar participants how she had been deeply despondent; she had no desire to read God's Word or pray. In the midst of a great void in her life she asked God, "What's wrong with me?"

Bo Whittington, young housewife and mother of two children, had been a church organist, taught Sunday School, and was faithful in attendance. Then a great dryness set in. In 1984 she and her husband moved to Atlanta, Georgia, and visited Eastside Baptist Church. After the service, she said to him, "These people are too happy and alive. They're not Southern Baptists." The next day she called the church to make sure. Sure enough it was!

Seeking to find the missing link in her life, she enrolled in a Continuing Witness Training class. When she heard the first probing question about heaven and eternity, she was unsure about her salvation. Bo wiped a tear away; "Pride kept me from admitting my uncertainty." Her equipper presented the gospel as they went out. She wrote her own testimony as the training progressed, using all the right words. The uncertainty grew stronger.

One day she realized, while in her home, that if she died she would be cast into the lake of fire, as described in the Book of Revelation. Bo imagined her two sons walking around heaven asking, "Where's my mommy?" Pride and the devil no longer stood in her way. She received Jesus as Savior.

A smile came back to her face as she exclaimed, "Since then it's been 'wall to wall' Jesus in my life!" God immediately gave her a burden to witness to the lost. "It's neat to share and see their faces when it clicks. We can all share."

Her voice trembled as she recounted a week-long mission trip to Worcester, Massachusetts in 1985 with 350 members of Eastside Church. During one of her prayer times prior to going, an impression came "Pray for John Nesbitt." She wrote his name in her Bible, began to pray for him, and told others. Their response, "What did you say? Do what?" In Massachusetts they visited door to door, distributing Scriptures and witnessing. Some led daytime children's ministries.

On her last morning in Worcester, a car stopped to ask directions as she distributed Scriptures. The man asked her name. "Bo. It's really short for Bonita. And your name?" "Jack. But that's a nickname also. My real name is John. John Nesbitt!" She broke into tears as she opened her Bible and showed him his name written inside. Nesbitt, from England, also wept as she presented the gospel and led him to Christ.

Tears returned as she relived the events. She finished her story, "I could have used a tract, but because of memorizing Scripture and a way to present Jesus, I just shared my heart. The Holy Spirit is more powerful than anything."

The four-day crusade led by Bo's pastor, Clark Hutchinson, drew four thousand people and resulted in 176 professions of faith in a city local Christians called "the graveyard of evangelism"!

Jerry Vines, former president of the Southern Baptist Convention and co-pastor of First Baptist Church in Jacksonville, Florida, says the spiritual battles of the eighties and nineties will be won on doorsteps. The big question is, in his words, "Who will be on the doorsteps . . . the communists, the cultists, or those who know the Savior?"

Jacob and Martha

The testimony of two at Lafayette Baptist Church in Fayetteville, North Carolina made me want to shout, "Listen, church. Here are some real-life answers to some real-life problems.

Meet Martha Seals, mother of three and a housewife. During her formative years Martha was exposed to alcohol, drugs, and other negative influences. Her mother taught her about Jesus and she became a Christian at fourteen. Married at fifteen, her husband was only eighteen. They began married life traveling in the Army. Eight years later both realized that unless Christ became the center of their home, they would have no home.

Shortly after Martha and her husband moved to Fayetteville, they joined Lafayette Baptist Church. Her pastor, Frank Page, began training her to witness. She says of him, "Our pastor has a deep love for the souls of men and women." She hastens on, "Soul-winning has changed my whole life. Once I thought I had no real meaning or purpose in life, that no one cared, but knowing Jesus and sharing Him with lost people changed all that. I thank God for His love and I thank Him also for a pastor like Frank Page. It is through the leadership of men like him, God directing, that laypersons will learn and grow into the people God has called us to be!"

Martha goes to a shopping center. God arranges an encounter with a Muslim. He gives his testimony, even talks about Christ, and invites her to share her beliefs about Him. In her backyard, over the fence, she shares the plan of salvation with three people. She tells of other opportunities. Then she makes this statement about her church, "It's been a home I've been able to grow in, grow into the healthy person God wants me to be, spiritually and emotionally. I have learned to love and work with other people who have the same hurts and needs as I. My desire is to help others. Jesus is Lord in our fellowship and not persons. The result is Bible-believing preaching and teaching with an outreach of soul-winning."

Jacob Hoff is fifty-three years old, the father of three daughters. He was raised with the dread influence of alcohol. As a boy he became a Christian during a week-long revival. His family and the church are the center points of his life. He says, "I experience much joy through teaching Sunday School, ministering as a deacon, and serving in various capacities in the church. However, the greatest joy comes from sharing Christ with others. That's the top floor of my Christian experience. I sense the best is yet to come. I want to walk on a steady upward plane till I go home." Jacob laments that he was called to be a witness many years ago, but responded only recently when he became involved in CWT. His favorite verse of Scripture is Luke 15:7 "I tell you, there will be more joy in heaven over one sinful person who repents than over ninety-nine upright people who do not need any repentance" (Williams).

There have been more CWT training seminars for pastors and church leaders in North Carolina than any other state. While baptism figures were declining across the Southern Baptist Convention, North Carolina had an increase in 1985. The commitment of Richard Everett, personal evangelism director for North Carolina, to the CWT process and its potential is a major factor in that growth. Frank Page has assisted Everett in his own church and on the state and national level.

Everett is personally responsible for a number of seminary and Bible college students being trained in personal evangelism. He constantly enlists pastors and laymen, and states, "If there's anything more important in God's kingdom than witnessing and teaching others to do so, God has not revealed it to me."

Page is now pastor of Gambrell Street Baptist Church in Fort Worth, Texas, having received a call to go there in late 1987.

Drew

Forty-three-year-old Drew Allen stood just outside the doorway and continued his testimony; "I was a bum and nearly drove my wife out of her mind. Jesus saved me three years ago and everything changed. I learned what it means to really love my wife. All those wrong things I did before are gone. Christ has taken over my life. Jesus will change you and save you, too." The man considered as Drew presented the gospel. He was saved. Allen is a simple man with limited education. It was evident he had memorized the gospel presentation. It was also abundantly clear as he wove his testimony throughout, that Christ is alive in his heart and life.

A few minutes later the man's wife drove into the carport with her thirteen-year-old daughter. Drew greeted her and said to the husband, "Tell your wife." The husband informed her he had given his life to Christ. Immediately turning his attention to the mother Drew asked, "Are you sure you'll go to heaven when you die?" She was. Drew then inquired about the daughter who had gone inside. He talked to her also. He missed no one in the house!

Harold Hudson is Drew's pastor. Their church is Westside Baptist in Jacksonville, Florida. Hudson has led the church since 1973 when their Sunday School attendance was just over one hundred and their budget thirty thousand dollars. The membership has gone from three hundred to near three thousand and the budget to $2 million in that period of time. They baptized ten in 1973. It was 426 in 1985. Sunday School attendance has soared to twelve hundred a week.

Westside is a church filled with miracle-believing, miracle-receiving prayer warriors, witnesses, and disciplers! As many as two hundred members come to pray for those who go on scheduled visitation. When the owner of property adjacent to the church refused to sell, one-hundred fifty prayers warriors lined the fence separating the property and ask God to clear the way. Within weeks a portion of the property was available. (Can you imagine looking out your window and seeing people on their knees all along your fence, praying?) The walls of the sanctuary were literally knocked out to build more seating space. In 1988 construction on a new auditorium began. It will seat twenty-five hundred with plans for expansion later to thirty-five hundred.

When we discuss figures and baptisms some people poke fun saying "All you do is count nickels and noses." Each nose has a soul behind it. It takes nickels and dollars to minister, witness, preach, disciple, and teach. Another complaint one hears when we talk about growth is, "My church is small. That doesn't apply to me." Westside was a small church just over a decade ago.

This church did't just happen. Hudson had to lead, equip, preach, and be the point man. He has homegrown most of his own staff, onetime laymen in the church, who now work side by side with him.

Want to know how to grow a church? Ask Harold!

Want to know if witnessing is fun? Ask Drew!

8
Treasure Maps

Faithful is he that calleth you, who also will do it (1 Thess. 5:24).

They that wait upon the Lord shall renew their strength; they shall mount up with wings like eagles; they shall run, and not be weary; and they shall walk, and not faint (Isa. 40:31).

Treasure Maps

During the period from 1980-85 all was not roses in my life. God allowed me to see miracle stacked on miracle. He also allowed the rain to fall. Lawsuits emerged from the ill-fated Augusta radio station which was declared bankrupt. I made a vain attempt to settle the dispute by bringing all parties together and fashioning an offer to those we owed. It was insufficient. Lawyers fees mounted. At times I fell into great despondency. The oil business collapsed. Our investments there turned to ashes! I didn't have the money to pay off the debt which now was way beyond $600,000. I kept asking God, "Why God? Why this? I've turned my life completely over to You. I believe I'm in Your will. What more do You want?" I was to learn later.

I had made the million dollars. It was now slipping through my hands like sand. Income was practically nil. Living expenses and debts had to be paid. All efforts on my part to end the long nightmare with a personal settlement came to naught until finally, at the end of 1985 the lawyers found a way to effect a compromise in my case. When we paid the agreed amount, there was very little cash left, our home was gone, and I was in a state of shock. For three months I literally ran from the world. I took leave of any assignments from the Home Mission Board and retreated as far back into my shell as possible, trying to sort out my dilemma.

As I reflected and prayed, God began to speak. Don't ask me to explain how He speaks. You just know! He wanted me to trust Him, not a bank account, oil wells, or interest on money, or anything else. And the test came when He said, "You trusted Me when you had the million dollars and enough for the rest of your life (you thought). Will you trust Me less now that all material things are gone? Do you really care about lost people? Do you really love Me? Or has this been a great charade, just so many words and show?" Decision time came.

Satan entered the picture, "If you go back into secular work, you can make the million all over again. You'll never make any money as a witness or teacher. In fact, you just might starve! This whole scene is a mirage, a vapor. Let's get swinging with the money making!"

God had allowed me to see too much of Him to move out of His will! In the decade from 1975-85, I had seen multiplied hundreds of laypersons, pastors, and staff personnel across the face of the earth, boldly telling others about Jesus. The untold miracles of salvation flooded my mind. I realized that nothing on the face of the earth could have a more lasting impact in eternity than being a witness and encouraging and training others to do the same. I said, "Lord, unless You tell me plainly to do something else, I'm continuing in the Mission Service Corps. What I eat, or wear, where I live, whether I have much or little of this world's goods, all is in Your hands! I belong to You."

One of the most innovative ideas developed by Southern Baptists in recent years is the Mission Service Corps. Had it not been for this concept, I would not have been so deeply involved as a layperson in ministry.

This full-time volunteer arm of the SBC is open to anyone: layperson, pastor, preacher, church staff member, male or female, young or old. Talents and skills of a hundred kinds are used to support witness, ministry, and mission efforts throughout America and across the world. In 1989, there were eleven-hundred Mission Service Corps personnel on active duty.

Howard

During a conference in South Carolina, a pastor troubled by difficulties of bringing new converts into his fellowship, said, "We've gone out and won a number of people to Christ. But we don't baptize very many of them. Why?" The question surfaces often.

Dr. Howard Ramsey, a man who has encouraged and held me up through the years, addressed the question in Atlanta as he spoke to gathered evangelism directors from over the nation. He said, "You are to be a part of making disciples, marking them and maturing them. Leading someone to Christ is only the beginning of the Great Commission. We must go, not only to lead them to Christ, but to gather them into the local fellowship. Whatever it takes to accomplish that, do it."

Ramsey is a man who can see a lost world. He's a person with one objective: Reach as many as possible as soon as you can for the time is short. Witness, teach others to do so as you go with them, bring in those who are saved, teach and disciple them, and repeat the process over and over again.

He tells of being saved in a small Texas church committed to helping Christians grow. He was already out of college and busy in the professional world. Deacon Johnny Yates had the responsibility of Ramsey's follow-up care. Yates taught him to pray, the importance of daily Bible study, and regular church attendance. Through the organizations of the church he was led to tithe and give offerings. And he learned to love lost souls and how to share the gospel with them. The deacon and his pastor, Cordell Bales, were carrying out the Great Commission in his life. Little did they know this young man of twenty-seven would become a pastor and lead four churches in modeling what he had seen in their lives. Or that he would become an evangelism leader with influence that rings throughout the world. It all began with a pastor who led Ramsey to Christ. And a deacon who discipled.

Prayer, Bible study, and selling out to Jesus by word and action will place us in a position to receive what God has in store for each of us. He has more for us than most ever dream possible. We must allow God to use us, as He in turn grows others. In the process we reach the lost. We grow spiritually as we do! Matthew 28:19-20 "Go then and make disciples of all the nations, baptize them into the name of the Father, the Son and the Holy Spirit, and teach them to practice all the commands that I have given you. And I myself will surely be with you all the days, down to the very close of an age" (Williams).

During late 1986, Dr. Ramsey lived through some hard days in his life. He underwent surgery. His wife, Lawanda, had been ill. His son-in-law developed a malignant brain tumor and his daughter was dying of cancer. With misty eyes I heard him say, "I pray God will give me as much concern for lost people as I now have for my own daughter." He was to preach her funeral. The true measure of Yates and Bales became clear that day. I was listening to a great soul-winner, a man who has had profound influence on my life, as well as many, many others, calling out to God for a measure of concern which few can understand.

Joy, Ramsey's daughter, had been practically estranged from her husband's family during most of the years of their marriage. During the days of her illness, God brought the family together again. She said to Howard, "You won't understand what I'm going to tell you as a daughter. As a pastor you will. Since this cancer has allowed me to be close to my husband's family and since they are listening to me talk about Jesus, I wouldn't trade the opportunity to be a witness to them and others for a clean bill of health."

Wherever he goes, day or night, Howard Ramsey tells others about Christ. Joy was well taught!

Johnny

Johnny Hunt is short, has wavy black hair and a dark complexion. He is of Indian heritage. He's in a hurry. When I met him he was pastor of Long Leaf Baptist Church in Wilmington, North Carolina.

His mother and father divorced when he was seven. His mother raised four boys and two girls. Johnny says of his early life, "I stayed in and out of trouble as a young teenager, drinking and gambling at the age of twelve. When I was sixteen years old I had a car accident and should have been killed. I quit school the day I turned sixteen to run a pool hall. I spent most of my time drinking and hustling pool. When I was eighteen I married Janet. After two years of a rocky marriage we began attending church (Long Leaf). After four weeks, I fell under conviction. A few weeks later I accepted Christ. He took away the desire to drink, gamble, and curse. He placed within my life a love for Him, His church, and all people. I was so excited about Christ I immediately began to tell my family and a few friends. Happiness came when I bragged on Jesus."

Johnny says he felt a compulsion to witness. Invitations to give his testimony at nearby churches resulted in God's call into the ministry. He answered that call and the results have been nothing short of miraculous. After finishing Bible college and seminary, he was ultimately called to be pastor of Long Leaf.

The year before he accepted the call, the church baptized fifteen. Five years later Long Leaf led the North Carolina Baptist Convention in baptisms. Sunday School attendance increased 400 percent. The church budget went from a hundred thousand dollars to nearly half-a-million dollars. This was a church which wasn't supposed to grow. It was in a community which had stopped growing. Nobody told Johnny!

It was a joy to go visiting with him. We were invited into a mobile home. There we found a couple, not married, living together. The man's divorce was not yet final. The woman held their baby in her arms. She was a Christian, but quickly acknowledged she was outside God's will and knew it. The young man accepted Christ as Savior. As we prepared to leave Johnny said, "Don't wait. Get into church now. Turn everything over to God. Begin anew this very minute." On our way back to the church Johnny told me, "Until Jesus has a chance to change lives, lives are never changed. We must take Christ to them first. We must deal with people where we find them, not where we'd like them to be." He told me he'd return and counsel with them in a few days. Johnny later married the couple.

Here was a man whose church was leading the state in baptisms. He was personally winning people to Christ and equipping his people to do so. (Pastor, do you understand?)

I saw Johnny next at Bible Baptist Institute in Graceville, Florida, where we were to train the largest group of people ever in one CWT seminar. One-hundred eighty were certified. In two nights of visitation with folks from local churches, the gospel was presented 254 times and sixty were saved! Revival fell on the students during the week. One of them was saved.

The day we arrived many of the students were exhausted because of exams. It took an additional hour just to register everyone. Attitudes were not the best. Departing from the schedule, I asked Johnny to preach. Before the week was over they asked him to preach during a special Thursday-evening service they had arranged. Revival fell on the place.

Hunt was called as pastor of First Baptist in Woodstock, Georgia in early 1987. He baptized more people that year, 318, than had been attending Sunday School the year before, 262! The first six months of the 1988 church year he baptized 438. Eight hundred were attending Sunday School. Forty witnessing teams were training and going out. Thirty acres of land had been purchased for future needs. Half a million dollars was raised in thirty days to pay for it. His bulletin said, "Full Sunday evening worship service." Mission giving had skyrocketed. His evangelism budget exceeded thirty thousand dollars. There's not a more exciting, effective young pastor in America today than Johnny Hunt. Johnny is on fire for Jesus!

As a pastor, you don't have to be a Johnny Hunt, a Norm Boshoff, or a Harold Hudson to grow a church. You have to be exactly who you are and sold out to Jesus. You must be an equipper and discipler of your people. You must be a role-model witness before your people. As a layperson you don't have to understand the Bible from cover to cover to witness. But you must also be sold out to Jesus. You must be willing to let God use you. You need some training. Whether you're a pastor or layperson, you must learn the truth that we are simply conduits for the message. The Holy Spirit does the work through us.

Six steps to the Spirit-controlled life are outlined in the third Bible lesson of the lay evangelism school materials copyrighted by the Home Mission Board of the Southern Baptist Convention. I include the basic outline with their permission. I am convinced if we learn the truth embodied here, accept and act on those truths and trust God, we will be witnesses. No formula does the job. Only dedication and commitment—total commitment.

1. Recognize the Holy Spirit lives within you permanently because of the new birth. 1 Corinthians 3:16: "Are you not conscious that you are God's temple, and that the Spirit of God has His permanent home in you?"
2. Realize that God's expressed will is for you to be controlled, to be filled (completely controlled) by His Spirit. Ephesians 5:18: "But ever be filled with the Spirit."
3. Genuinely desire to be controlled by the Spirit. John 7:37: "If anyone is thirsty, let him come to me and drink."
4. Deal with sin. 1 John 1:9: "If we confess our sins, He is to be depended on, since He is just, to forgive our sins and to cleanse us from every wrong."
5. Abandon your will to God's will. Galatians 2:20: "I have been crucified with Christ, and I myself no longer live, but Christ is living in me; the life I now live as a mortal man I live by faith in the Son of God who loved me and gave Himself for me."
6. Receive the fullness of the Spirit through faith. Luke 11:-13: "So if you, in spite of your being bad, know how to give your children what is good, how much more surely will your Father in heaven give the Holy Spirit to those who continue to ask Him?" (Williams).

Many, many years after I became a Christian I began to understand these truths. They can literally revolutionize one's Christian life!

Max

The day Mickie and I made our commitment to full-time Christian service through the Mission Service Corps, Max Cadenhead was guest preacher at West Bradenton Baptist Church. Max put his arms around us and prayed. He and I were to work together for two years. About a year after we went to the Home Mission Board, Max accepted the call as pastor of

First Baptist Church in Naples, Florida. Just before going he told me, "I've got to put into practice what I've been telling everybody else to do all these months and years."

He was humble. Cadenhead had already put to practice the essentials of growth in a number of difficult places. He had built a great, growing church in the small community of Dover, east of Tampa. The same had happened in the suburbs of Detroit, Michigan.

Max had a spinal cancer operation two months before we were to do a Lay Evangelism School in Naples in 1986. We didn't know his real condition and were deeply concerned. Instead of an attitude of defeat, we found him praising God and living in complete victory.

There had been difficult growing pains during the four years he had been in Naples. Growth involves pain. His daughter had been through a bout with drugs, a long bout, one filled with heartache, tears, and heartrending setback and disappointment. Cindy, in her twenties, was back home, still in protracted rehab. Max's wife Doris, a godly woman, was ministering to the needs of her family as well as the church.

When Cadenhead went to Naples the church was burdened by a staggering debt. Sunday School attendance had been declining for years. Baptisms were near an all-time low of seventeen the past year. During the first four years of his ministry, baptisms averaged seventy-five per year, church membership grew by over five hundred, Sunday School attendance was up, total receipts went from over three-hundred thousand dollars to more than twice that in 1986. Dollars for missions more than doubled and the debt was in hand.

Remember his statement, "I've got to put into practice all these things I've been telling others to do all these months and years"? He had done it.

He preached the president's sermon at the Florida Baptist Convention the month after we were in his church. Cindy sang a beautiful Christian hymn afterward. His fellow pastors and friends gave him a standing ovation as he, his son Jerry, Cindy, and Doris embraced on stage.

How would I describe Max? He works hard. He is a fearless preacher, true to God's Word. He loves people. He is a teacher. He is a witness. He is a discipler. He loves the Lord. And, he works hard!

Preston

Preston Bailey is rather frail looking, until he speaks. Go with me to a community of thirty-two hundred seven miles west of Blytheville, Arkansas. There's an Air Force base nearby so people are moving in and out all the time; not an easy place to build a church. Preston has a map with the name of every person in Gosnell noted. A special symbol tells him if a person listed is a member of his church. When his people get ready to go out, he simply hands them a block and says "Go get 'em." CWT is the centerpiece of his witness training.

The first year in Gosnell he baptized thirty-three, the next year sixty-seven, and in 1985 he baptized eighty-three and was thirteenth in the state of Arkansas! You just aren't supposed to be able to do that in a place like Gosnell. One pulpit committee from a rather staid old Southern Baptist church talked to him. Needless to say, he shook them up. Action is his middle name.

A few months before I was in Preston's church he led a teenage devil worshiper to Jesus. We went to see the young man's mother. It was my turn to lead. Not two minutes into our conversation, the father, in answer to one of my questions, said, "I know what you're here for and I know what you're going to say. My mind is made up. It's not going to change no matter what you say."

Stopped momentarily, I ask him if I might share with his wife. He said, "Go ahead." I presented the gospel. The father heard every word. Near the conclusion, the teenage son came in, clean-cut, neat, and bright. The mother delayed a decision. I asked her, "Did it make any difference in the life of your son when he accepted Jesus?" "Oh," she replied, "As much difference as night is from day." I posed a final question, "Don't you think God is trying to tell you something?" She joined her son in God's kingdom.

Turning to Bailey I asked if he'd like to add anything. Off he went on a ten-minute dissertation on how he knew God is real. It began with his own testimony. He then quoted scientists, historians, astronomers, and theologians. We were spellbound. He pointed out the sun is 93 million miles from earth. If it were further away, we'd freeze; closer, we'd burn up. The moon averages 240,000 miles from earth. If it were any closer, the tides would inundate all land. The earth is tilted at a twenty-three degree angle in relation to the sun. A few degrees change either way and life as we know it would not exist on earth. Winding down, Bailey concluded, "And who decided that man needed an eye. Or two of them!" Turning to the father I said, "That's one of the most interesting things I've ever heard." By this time he was just a shade warmer. Half growling he muttered, "I agree with you. But I'm not going to change my mind."

Preston Bailey learned some tough witnessing lessons on the streets of Fort Worth while attending Southwestern Seminary. One night about 9:30, alone on a witness assignment, he met four black youths in a tough section of the city. They crowded the sidewalk. God led in the encounter. "I see you like black power" he said to the leader who had a fist symbol on his T-shirt. A mean voice answered, "Yeah, that's right. What about it?" Preston said he could tell them about power greater than black power. Attention attained, he presented Jesus. When he asked the leader to kneel on the dirty sidewalk and pray, the

response was, "On this sidewalk?" "Yes, right here." All four
accepted Christ as Savior.

You read this and possibly think, *But, I'm not Preston and
I can't do that.*

Dr. Stephen Olford told me, "Some are evangelists. All can
be and are commanded to be witnesses." A fair interpretation
of Acts 1:8 tells me we are without excuse if we fail to witness.
Jesus is speaking, "You are going to receive power when the
Holy Spirit comes upon you, and you must be witnesses for me
in Jerusalem and all over Judea and Samaria, and to the very
ends of the earth" (Williams). Jesus didn't say debate about it,
think long, or consider. He said you must be witnesses.

You and I are not Preston Bailey. We are ourselves. God can
use any of us.

Gary

Two staff members rushed into Gary Taylor's study.
"Preacher have you heard the news? One of our seven-year-old
students was shot by her mother last night. A sister and brother
are dead!" They rushed to the hospital and found the child
wrapped in bandages with life-support systems attached. The
doctor's prognosis; "There's no hope for her. We believe she
won't make it." She died. A distraught, confused, depressed
mother had killed her three children.

This single-parent family had lived a few blocks from Tower
Grove Baptist Church in the midst of one of Saint Louis, Missouri's evolving, continually changing communities. Most of
the homes were built years ago. A large park across the street
from the church was a haven for homosexuals.

Two days after the little girl died, Taylor received a call
asking him to visit the mother in jail. He went. There he found
a frail, small woman in anguish and mental pain. Out of a
background of utter despair, she had tried to rear the three

children, each of whom had a different father. After being with her for nearly an hour, realizing she knew the awfulness of what had happened, this caring preacher led her to the Lord. A guard motioned for him to leave. The small, wisp of a woman put her arms around him and said, "Oh preacher, I wish I'd found your church before last Wednesday!" He took two steps toward the door, turned back with tears streaming down his face, and said, "Oh, Lavinia, forgive me, my church, and my people that we didn't find you before last Wednesday!"

I met Taylor at Glorieta in August, 1987, during a CWT seminar. There was no trace of the mammoth difficulties he had encountered in that ministry, only an affirmation that God was blessing. Two weeks later I was to learn the measure of this man.

During an associational pastor's conference I attended, he told of a rainstorm eighteen months before which had dumped four inches of water on the roof of the sanctuary and educational building while repairs were being made. Water had poured in. Discovering asbestos in the ceilings, bids were taken to remove it. The lowest was $350,000. Work began. Massive repairs and remodeling took place. The church now had a debt near $2 million. An offer of a hundred thousand dollars was made to settle by one insurance company. The congregation was struggling simply to pay the interest. Sunday School attendance had dropped from a thousand to around eight hundred. Some of the deacons had given up and left. Gary Taylor's voice broke as he told his fellow pastors, "We're not quitting. Even though this last year has been the most difficult in my twenty-five years of ministry, we're not giving up. I don't know what will happen, but we must stay. Someone has to be at the door of hell as a stopgap." He paused and added, "Ten thousand years from now only one thing will matter." Sweeping his arm in a wide arc toward the homes and park outside he concluded, "Were these saved? Did we witness to them?" As I looked about, a number of pastors whose churches had helped Tower Grove were fighting back tears. So was I. Just before he sat down he quoted Galatians 6:9, "And let us not be weary in well doing: for in due season we shall reap, if we faint not."

Later in the week he and I visited a young lady who had been attending worship services. He presented the gospel, prayed for her, and asked her to receive God's priceless gift. Her response, "I want to, but I can't right now." He reviewed the Scriptures and asked again. Still she refused. As we parked at the church, he looked at me, "We must pray for Brenda." And pray he did, breaking into tears over her lost soul. Walking into the church I prayed, too. "Oh, Lord, that I might have a heart heavy for people and their souls as Gary Taylor does! Lord give me the fullness of that indomitable Spirit that refuses to grow weary. Precious Savior, let me see the lost about me with such compassion that I cannot but share You. Thank You, Lord, for the ministry in my life of this humble, dedicated preacher."

In the midst of great burdens and problems Tower Grove has continued to baptize near a hundred or more each year.

Before leaving I asked Taylor what it would take to turn Southern Baptists and the Christian church around. He gave me a three-pronged answer. "First, pastors must quit being ecclesiastical bishops and desk jockeys. We must knock on doors and model concern for lost souls by being witnesses. We must equip and lead our people into the harvest. Secondly, we must not only believe the Bible, we must act on it. Do what God commands. The only thing worse than dead liberalism is dead fundamentalism." Finally Taylor said, "In my evangelism class at seminary, my assignment was to write a paper. Writing papers will never get the job done. Evangelism must be experienced and practiced by seminary students in the streets and on the doorsteps of lost people everywhere they go."

One year later while flying to Saint Louis for another seminar in Taylor's church, I found him conducting a funeral service.

Soon after greeting me he beamed, "You should have been with me this morning. I presented the gospel during the funeral; four people were saved at the conclusion." It was to be another glorious week!

There were thirty-nine in our seminar. August's furnace-like heat soared to 104 degrees. As our nineteen teams visited they found families who had no air conditioning sitting on porches and steps. God moved them out where we could find them. Forty-two were saved! The following Sunday morning the aisles of Tower Grove were filled with people at invitation time as ten made public their professions of faith. Others rededicated their lives to Jesus. Trained CWT witnesses assisted Gary with those who came forward. God sent real revival! Gary said the church goal for the new year was two-hundred baptisms. With God's help he pledged to lead one person a week to the Lord and baptize that person. Staff members had their own personal goals.

I asked about Brenda, the young lady he had wept over. A broad smile covered his face, "I baptized her and her roommate. Both were saved." The tragic story of Lavinia, the young mother who had killed her three children continued. She was serving 101 years in prison. Gary corresponded with her monthly. His love for people, saved or lost, is itself a miracle!

America's Heartland

Southern Baptist missionaries reach out across the world to over a hundred countries seeking to bring the lost to Christ and establish churches. And well they should. The lost need Christ in Africa, Korea, Brazil, Japan, or wherever they are. Yet, only three countries on earth have more lost people than we do here in America. And the lost are literally on the doorsteps of Southern Baptist churches.

In September, 1987, I spent two weeks with Roy Moody,

evangelism director of Kansas-Nebraska. We crisscrossed the state of Kansas, with our first stop in Topeka. There during his evangelism conference we were inspired and challenged by Joel Gregory, Darrell Robinson, D L. Lowery, Leonard Hinton, James Smith, Milton Ferguson, and Esther Burroughs.

Weeks earlier Moody and a number of key directors of missions had enlisted pastors and laypersons for regional lay evangelism schools in Topeka and Garden City, Kansas. The first evening eighty were in attendance. An air of expectancy prevailed. Each afternoon the teaching staff visited lost prospects. Mark Patton, host pastor at First Southern, Topeka, asked me to visit a lady in her seventies. "She's gone home to die. I understand she's lost," he said. We found her seemingly asleep at a nursing home. I asked questions as she stirred. Within fifteen minutes she clasped my hand, prayed, and settled her eternal destiny with Jesus Christ.

The following afternoon Roy Moody visited a couple who had made professions of faith days earlier. They began to tell their friends immediately what had happened. One became so interested she wanted to know more! Roy led the friend the Christ. (Isn't it strange that new Christians tell others about Christ and what has happened to them while many of the rest of us can't seem to open our mouths?)

The following afternoon my team surveyed the street adjacent to the church. We received a cold reception at the first house. A teen took a tract at the next house. We met a man returning from work in the next driveway. One of our team members began to share Jesus. He stopped us, saying he had to go inside to care for an elderly parent. Turning to leave he said, "We can't visit your church. Our time is all taken by this responsibility." A golden opportunity for ministry was discovered on the church doorsteps. A few steps away we met a man in his twenties in the yard. Jay Brown presented the gospel to him. He committed his life to Christ. Next door Cecil Rambo, a layperson from Alabama, presented Jesus to a lady as they stood on the sidewalk. In one hour, next to the church, we were able to present the gospel twice, leave a tract, and see one person come to Christ.

Multiplied thousands would be saved if we would start at the doorsteps of our churches across America, present and gospel, and tell people we love them. The fields truly are "white unto harvest." The nagging question is, Where are the witnesses?

Fifty went visiting in our school. People were saved, Christians equipped, and everyone was excited about Jesus!

The following day Moody and I drove west 350 miles to Garden City. Moving across the wide, rolling vistas of eastern Kansas, we settled onto the plains where cattle, grain elevators, oil wells, and fields covered the landscape. When we arrived, Randy Caddell, host pastor, was busy ministering to families of a tragic car wreck that had killed three and left others injured. He had been at Garden City First Southern only five weeks. From a low point of sixty in Sunday School there were 110 attending the Sunday I was with them. A tremendous outpouring filled the aisles during invitation time. Four accepted Jesus, four others joined, twenty-one made commitments to witness and openly confessed, some weeping openly. A deacon said to Caddell, "I've been wrong. Forgive me. I'll support you and this church in whatever it does!" Caddell looked to his counselors for help. Most were coming forward themselves. Twenty-four who responded attended the first session of our lay evangelism school.

Moody prayed and asked God to save people every day. Monday I led a maid to the Lord at the motel. Tuesday night a couple, disturbed after hearing the first Bible lesson on The New Life, settled it all by accepting Christ at 10:30 PM. Wednesday the pastor led a young man to Christ while counseling. Five came forward at the beginning of our Wednesday night teaching session! Thursday afternoon Roy and I surveyed a street adjacent to the church. At the fifth house a woman in her sixties greeted us, "You're just the men I want to see. I don't understand God. I'm living on Social Security and just getting by. My former husband divorced me seventeen years ago. He has plenty. Why? Why?" Moody responded, then asked if we could share the real answer to the problems in her life. Within a few minutes she accepted Christ and prayed, "Thank You, God, for saving me. I've wanted to do this for a long, long time."

Fifty-one attended our first session Monday evening. Forty-six went visiting Friday night. Seven were saved. Most of the laypersons had never shared Christ before. The reporting session and celebration went on until 10:45. Nine pastors and ten laypersons were equipped to teach. Many prayed for God's power and movement in our midst. Roy Moody worked diligently with Andy St. Andres, director of missions, preparing for the week. God's people were revived, souls were saved, everyone got excited, the result of praying, preparing, and going!

Since Jesus Himself walked dusty pathways speaking to the lost and touching hurting people the plan has not changed. We are to *go!*

The following week I ran into a buzz saw in a Midwestern state. Preparation was minimal. Pastors wanted to be certified to teach without fulfilling requirements. We prayed together, seeking God's face. The situation improved. One who decided to pay the price in preparation had a visitor from his Sunday service approach him in a restaurant. "Preacher, I've just got to know how to be saved." After leading him to Christ he discovered everyone else in the family was lost, went to his house on visitation night, and led another to Jesus.

As I had done in both churches in Kansas, I decided to survey the block adjacent to the church. The pastor and I visited his next-door neighbor whom he had befriended. The seventy-year-old man listened intently as I presented the gospel, allowed me to clear some hang-ups and concluded, "I know going to church and doing good works won't save me." He bowed his head and Christ paved his way into eternity. He had been waiting for someone to tell him how to be saved. In three churches, hundreds of miles apart, we led people to Christ within a block of each sanctuary. Most of us don't know where to go to witness. Try next door to your church.

Revival, Sure Enough!

In 1986 Tom Kyzer, who was to become my pastor later, expressed deep concern that Sunday School attendance had shown a small decline and baptisms were down. I had known Tom for five years, having taught a lay evangelism school for Old Spanish Fort Baptist Church in the early eighties, soon after he arrived as pastor. Under his leadership the church had shown steady growth. In an expanding part of Baldwin County, Alabama, the opportunities were tremendous, in his words. And he desired God's continued blessings. He knew that God wanted him as under shepherd to lead. He was willing to plan, work, and inspire, and to go, equip, and weep with a heart broken for the lost. There was an obvious love unbounded for his people. As we finished our lunch he concluded, "I believe God wants this church to expand our reach of discipleship and evangelism. Everyone of us is to be involved in ministry and witness, but my people need more help with strategy, prospecting, and a host of other things." At that time he had two staff members, Dana Workman, music director and youth minister, and Ken Richardson, administrator and educational director.

How easy it would have been to make excuses and say it was just a temporary decline. That was not to be.

Because of Tom's warm wonderful spirit in the Lord and his keen interest in reaching people, Mickie and I decided to move our letter to Old Spanish Fort. We knew a number of members. It was ten miles closer than our former church.

Though I traveled extensively and was unable to be there often, I was to see in my home church another great revival, similar to what we had experienced at West Bradenton Baptist Church years earlier. These statistics show what happened.

	1983	1984	1985	1986	1987	1988
Baptisms	99	93	69	59	69	147
Average Sunday School Attendance	355	392	456	444	483	574

In early 1989, Sunday School attendance was nearing seven hundred.

Before the resurgence in growth a staff member was added, David Huggins, minister of evangelism and discipleship. Later Ricky Watt, part-time minister of youth, was called.

If you could ask the five staff members, including the pastor, Tom Kyzer, what contributed to the growth, here are some of the answers you'd receive.

"Our people are excited about Jesus. When people get excited about something, they are going to share it."

"Reaching people is a priority in everything we do . . . revivals, special music programs, youth get-togethers, socials . . . the purpose is not simply entertainment. It's reaching people for Jesus."

"The music really touches hearts. It is alive!"

"More and more of our people are comfortable with sharing the gospel as we use a tract, *Are You Sure?*, the New Testament itself, and Continuing Witness Training. We are not simply doing church visitation all the time. Witnessing is involved."

"There is a spirit of friendliness and caring when new Christians or visitors come. No matter who they are they feel accepted."

"The main thing is our warm, loving people."

"I believe our growth has been from God. I'm not sure we can explain it. I pray that God will continue and that we will be faithful in working for Him."

Tom would not say the preaching is moving and anointed dramatically by the Holy Spirit. I will!

Ken would not say Sunday School teaching and reaching is strong and biblical and a key ingredient. I will!

Dana would not say the choir is doing a greater job than ever before and because of the music worship is super. I will!

David would not say witnessing is the fulcrum around which all true outreach occurs. I will!

Ricky would not say the youth and I worship and have great fun together and we witness and we're in revival, too. I will!

Prayer meetings on Wednesday evening are truly prayer meetings. There's testimony to God's grace and love, requests for all kinds of intercession, praise, songs, and prayer, prayer in small groups led by deacons and corporate prayer. I would further say, "God is up to some glorious, marvelous, miraculous things. We simply need to get in on what he's up to."

Bruce and Roger

Bruce Adkins bowed his head and led the young mother to Jesus on her front steps. He shared follow-up material with her and moved toward the next house. Looking toward Roger Bedford, Sr., he said, "This one's yours." Bedford approached a teenager bouncing a basketball in the driveway. The clean-cut, fine-looking youngster clutched the basketball close as Roger asked questions and began the gospel. Open as a sponge, he consumed every word and gave his life to Christ. Adkins sent up prayers of praise as we drove to his home for supper.

I met Bruce, a church starter, earlier that day in Billings, Montana. He had proudly taken us to the building God had providentially provided for this, his latest church, and enthusiastically told of the solid start and initial growth. That turned out to be only the beginning of our visit. He wanted his friend Roger and me to witness with him on a street near the church. Obviously this was a church starter who knew one of the cornerstones of building churches was witness, witness, witness! He was refreshing. Bible classes, knocking on doors, and love were the ingredients for establishing a work.

Adkins moved to Montana from Arizona in the early eighties after retiring. He'd spent thirty years as a public accountant. The time had come to hunt game in Big Sky Country. In the midst of God's beautiful lands, the Lord reached down and called him out. Off to Southwestern Baptist Theological Seminary he went, no longer a young man. He arrived opposed to one-on-one witnessing. Many times he thought, *That's the wrong way to do it.* In his own words, "I didn't have an alternative." At Southwestern he met Dr. Roy Fish, professor of evangelism, and read his book, *Every Member Evangelism.* "My heart was broken. This really was it—personal witnessing. I began to step out in faith and God gave me vision and confidence. Now I'm hunting bigger game . . . the greatest of all . . . lost men, women, and young people."

After supper he drove back to the same street, walked to the next house, and said to me, "This one's yours." Underneath my breath I was pleasing the devil. "Surely after two in a row there won't be another. Anyway, it's cold and dark and late." A man in his sixties cracked the front door ever so slightly and snapped, "I've got company. Who are you and what do you want?" Telling him we were from nearby Pyramid church I asked for a few minutes of his time. He nodded and I eased into the gospel, not knowing how long he'd listen. Warming to the conviction of the Holy Spirit, he opened the door, and stood with us on the stoop. He gave his heart to Christ. Three houses next to each other on a street neither of us had ever been on before, three souls now in God's kingdom!

"You can't do that in Montana. It's different here." Roger and I heard those words a few days before in Havre, Montana, where we led a lay evangelism school. I observed Roger Bedford, an attorney and lay person from Russellville, Alabama, very closely during our week together. He witnessed to a motel clerk, the motel owner, three waitresses, a meat cutter, lady in a book store, a gas station attendant, two persons in the motel lobby, among others. Together, we presented the entire gospel to an immigration officer on the Canadian border.

On our way home, flying high above North Dakota, Roger shared his heart with me, "There's a difference from area to area in America, but it's of form and not substance. Down deep inside people are the same everywhere. In Alabama we lock in on fishing and the beach, skiing in Colorado, hunting in Montana, golf in Florida, and a million and one other distractions. As we look at life, secular or religious, the difference between success and failure is very subtle. It evolves around one's perspective of an obstacle. One views it as a stepping-stone, another as a stumbling block. Christians are very lax in developing their spiritual gifts and many will not follow the certain command of our Lord to be witnesses."

One of the great, great joys while criss-crossing America and other parts of the world during these ten years has been the inspiration and example of men like Bruce Adkins and Roger Bedford, Sr.

9
You *Can* Take It With You

Stop storing up your riches on earth where moths and rust make away with them, and where thieves break in and steal them. But keep on storing up your riches in heaven where moths and rust do not make away with them and where thieves do not break in and steal them. For wherever your treasure is, there too your heart will be (Matt. 6:19-21, Williams).

Then Jesus came up to them, and said, "Full authority in heaven and on earth has been given to me. Go then and make disciples of all the nations, baptize them into the name of the Father, the Son, and the Holy Spirit, and teach them to practice all the commands that I have given you. And I myself will surely be with you all the days, down to the very close of the age" (Matt. 28:18-20, Williams).

Robert Coleman, in *The Master Plan of Evangelism,* ended his great book with these words;

We are not living primarily for the present. Our satisfaction is in knowing that in generations to come our witness for Christ will still be bearing fruit through them in an ever widening cycle of reproduction to the ends of the earth and unto the end of time.

The world is desperately seeking someone to follow. That they will find someone is certain, but will he be a man who knows the way of Christ, or will he be one like themselves leading them only on into greater darkness?

This is the decisive question of our plan of life. The relevance of all that we do waits upon its verdict, and in turn, the destiny of the multitudes hangs in the balance.[1]

If you and I are to seriously impact our world for Christ, I believe we must fall to our knees as those dedicated men and women did in Colombia years ago, as the Koreans did at Yoido, and as our Jamaican brothers and sisters did in their all-night vigil, urgently calling upon God and beseeching Him to bring revival. Leonard Ravenhill said in his book, *Sodom Had No Bible,* "The church is dying on its feet because it is not living on its knees."[2]

Revival is desperately needed in America and across the world. Most of us who call ourselves Christian have become deadly cold and indifferent to the lost about us. The reason: we are cold and indifferent to God.

Stephen Olford wrote in *Heart-Cry for Revival*

> Revival is not some worked up excitement, it is rather an invasion from heaven that brings a conscious awareness of God.
>
> God's word comes alive. A study of revival shows that every visitation from heaven has brought with it a new interest in God's word. Great doctrines that were forgotten, or neglected, come to light; justification by faith, the forgiveness of sins, the work of the Spirit, the authority of the Bible, and the hope of the Lord's return.
>
> God's church comes alive. Christians cease to be passive and assume their true leadership in the family, the church, and the country. They become the 'salt' and the 'light' in contemporary society.
>
> God's work comes alive.[3]

As Stephen Olford wrote, we must have "an invasion from heaven." That invasion will bring us to a no-turning-back decision to break out of our lethargy as God leads. God is willing. God is ready. He is able. He waits on us. James tells us in chapter 4, verse 2 of his Epistle, "Ye have not, because ye ask not." If you want changes to take place in your Christian walk, tell God about it. Nothing will happen in our lives worth even one grain of salt in God's kingdom unless we make a decision to *move*. We must respond to God's call, one that has been sounded down through the ages. God spoke clearly in Isaiah 6:8, "I heard the voice of the Lord, saying, Whom shall I send, and who will go for us?" We must give the answer Isaiah gave, "Here am I; send me." Jesus said, "The laborers are few—I am the way—go ye therefore—ye must be my witnesses—ask and you shall receive." We truly stand without excuse. God's Word is plain.

The challenge issued by God's servants is clear. Two headlines in the *Florida Baptist Witness* trumpeted the call, "God May Be 'Withdrawing' From Southern Baptists" and "Evangelism Must Have Greater Priority."

Landrum Leavell, president of New Orleans Baptist Theological Seminary, has said, "God's blessings have been poured out on the Southern Baptist Convention in such great ways they can't even be measured. We are a revivalistic and evangelistic people whom God has blessed. When we get preoccupied with other things—God's hand will be withdrawn from us and God will find another people that He can use."

Jack Stanton, former first vice-president of the Southern Baptist Convention has said, "We will never win the world unless we go out into the world. The Bible doesn't command the lost to come to church. It commands the church to go to the sinners."

Dr. William Tanner, former president of the Southern Baptist Home Mission Board, stated as he resigned to return to Oklahoma as executive director, "The day of playing games is over. If we don't get serious about leading people to a saving knowledge of Jesus Christ, we're going to lose this country."

Dr. Howard Ramsey, director of personal evangelism for the

Home Mission Board, has said, "Across America, on an island here, another there, we are seeing exciting things happen as folks witness. But for the most part, we are failing tragically to carry the message of Jesus to lost people."

Darrell Robinson, vice-president, Evangelism, Home Mission Board, Southern Baptist Convention, says in his Broadman book *Total Church Life,*

> Every Christian is a minister. Some are involved as missionaries, evangelists, pastors, and teachers to the extent that they do not have to earn their bread through a "secular' job." Others earn their bread through a job and minister in a life-style for our Lord. The God-called leaders give oversight and equip the laity. The committed laity provides the great work force for fulfilling the ministry of the church. As they work together, the church is built up and the mighty work of God is accomplished.[4]

Richard Jackson, pastor of North Phoenix Baptist Church in Phoenix, Arizona, issues this challenge; "We're kidding ourselves. We get in our church houses and sing and pray and say, 'We're doing the good Lord's work." We say, 'Good News America, God Loves You,' and the world can't hear! If America is not going to hear us shout Good News America in our churches, they're going to have to hear it in the streets, in the schools and on the job." Jackson has baptized multiplied thousands in recent years. In 1988 North Phoenix gave more money to the Cooperative Program than any other church in the Southern Baptist Convention. He is eminently qualified to give us counsel and advice.

Dr. Charles Stanley, pastor of First Baptist Church in Atlanta and former president of the SBC, says, "For centuries we've gone to church and said, 'Choir sing, preacher pray, preacher preach, preacher shut up and let me go home.' If you've got God inside you and you don't tell others, there's something wrong. When you're not telling, you're choking off God's

Spirit. It affects your spirit and your body. When you're down and start talking about Jesus, something happens inside."

Dr. Bill Hogue, former evangelism director for the Southern Baptist Home Mission Board, sees the church this way, "The church is busy with itself, teaching itself, preaching to itself, receiving from self, building for self, and being pleased with self. Spiritual equipment for evangelism is a daily relationship to God and a continuing indwelling power of the Holy Spirit. Your equipment to evangelism is in your time with the Master and your submission to the Lordship of Christ thru the indwelling of the Holy Spirit."[5]

Vance Havner, that preacher of renown who went to be with the Lord recently, said, "Christ is a person and He reaches other persons through persons, not merely through plans and propaganda. We are propagandizing the faith instead of propagating it."

Elton Trueblood wrote many years ago in his book *The Company of the Committed,*

> There is no possibility of a genuine renewal of the life of the Church in our time unless the principle of universal witness is accepted without reservation. The struggle against apathy is so great a task that if we are to achieve even a semblance of a victory we cannot be satisfied to leave Christian work to the ordained clergymen.[6]

Again, let us hear Dr. Stephen Olford:

> It is my conviction that we will never have revival until God has brought the Church of Jesus Christ to a point of desperation. As long as Christian people can trust religious organization, material wealth, popular preaching, shallow evangelism, and promotional drives, there will never be revival. But when confidence in the flesh is smashed, and the church comes to the realization of her desperate wretchedness, blindness, and nakedness before God, then and only then will God break in![7]

Forrest "Woody" Watkins, former director of evangelism for the Tennessee Baptist Convention, stated in a letter to me:

> God has called every believer to be a life-style witness. Although God has given talents to each believer in His physical birth, He also has imparted gifts in His spiritual birth. Therefore, there would be differences in talents and gifts in each believer to be used for the glory of God. However, each believer is told to be a witness with what he has and give a witness everywhere. There should be no exceptions.

These men of God have spent lifetimes preaching, teaching, and witnessing. I believe we must accept their statements as truth because they are true to God's commands and His Word. If that is the case, what is our problem?

Lewis A. Drummond, writer, president of Southeastern Seminary, and former Billy Graham Professor of Evangelism at Southern Seminary in Louisville, Kentucky, expressed himself with conviction in the following statement included in a letter to me.

> Motivation in the Christian experience is an illusive quality, at least so it seems in our churches today. Pastors and lay leaders alike all but beg people to get involved in the task of ministry and service, and especially to become a personal witness for Jesus Christ. All agree that the task of evangelism is everybody's responsibility, but so few seem to actively involve themselves in the grand enterprise.

> Why is it that in the light of all the sermons, books, conferences, seminars, and every other communicated means employed, so few seem to commit themselves to be a personal witness for Christ? Perhaps we have been approaching the whole concept of motivating people to do personal evangelism from the wrong perspective. I may even go so far as to

say perhaps we have seen the whole motivation issue from an incorrect perspective.

The question that I wish to raise is this: Does God expect us to motivate people? In one sense of the word, of course, the answer is in the affirmative. God does use His people to motivate others. But that is not the primary source of motivation. It seems to me, in light of all the Scriptures state, that motivation essentially emanates from the presence and power of the Holy Spirit. God Himself, by his Holy Spirit, is the great Motivator. In reality, we cannot motivate people on any sustained basis to do Christian ministry but for a very short period. I have become convinced through the years of Christian ministry myself that if the Spirit of God does not genuinely grip a life, motivate that life, and then thrust that life out into personal witnessing, no sustained effort is ever forthcoming.

Dr. Drummond concluded, "Five simple words ought to be in every dedicated Christian's vocabulary for themselves, as well as to enable others to experience the fullness of the Holy Spirit." They are,

Acknowledge—your need.
Abandon—your sins.
Abdicate—the control of your life.
Ask—constantly.
Accept—the fact of the Spirit's fullness.

In an earlier chapter I covered in detail the "how to" of Dr. Drummond's five steps.

As I reflect on these profound statements by God's servants, my first reaction is to fall on my face and cry as Isaiah did, "Woe is me! for I am undone" (6:5).

I believe unless we come to that point of desperation Dr. Olford so aptly described, nothing will happen in your life or mine. We must face the foe head-on. Paul told us in Ephesians 6:12, "For our contest is not with human foes alone, but with the rulers, authorities, and cosmic powers of this dark world; that is, with the spirit-forces of evil challenging us in the heavenly contest." In the next few verses Paul provided the ammunition needed by each Christian for what is truly all-out war!

> So you must take on God's full armor, so as to be able to take a stand in the day when evil attacks you, and, after having completely finished the contest, to hold your own. Hold your position then, with your waist encircled with the belt of truth, put on right-doing as a coat of mail, and put on your feet the preparation the good news of peace supplies. Besides all these, take on the shield which faith provides, for with it you will be able to put out all the fire-tipped arrows shot by the evil one, take the helmet salvation provides, and take the sword the Spirit wields, which is the word of God. Keep on praying in the Spirit, with every kind of prayer and entreaty, at every opportunity (vv. 13-18).

Would you join me in claiming victory over all the forces of evil that would keep us from moving out in God's army, telling our neighbors, friends, and the world about Christ? For move we must or our world may be lost!

Dear Lord, forgive me for being weak, timid, and afraid. I know You have provided everything I need to overcome the snares of the devil. In Your Word You tell me I can do all things, everything You desire of me, every last thing, through You. Oh, Lord, I need help! Cleanse me that I may be a perfect vessel. Lord fill me with Your presence. Give me the power I need. Lord I commit all that I am, all that I have, all I ever hope to be into Your hands, no longer to trust self, but to trust only You. Lord, so fill and teach me that I will no longer be able to remain silent. Through Your strength, in the power of the Holy Spirit, which I claim, I will go and I will be a witness. Thank-

You, Lord for hearing and answering my prayer, in Jesus' precious name.

My God shall supply all your need according to his riches in glory by Christ Jesus (Phil. 4:19).

Stop storing up your riches on earth where moths and rust make away with them . . . . Keep on storing up your riches in heaven where moths and rust do not make away with them (Matt. 6:19, 21, Williams).

You *can* take it with you!

Notes

1. Robert Coleman, *Master Plan of Evangelism* (Old Tappan, N.J.: Fleming H. Revell Co., 1964) n.p.n. Used by permission.

2. Leonard Ravenhill, *Sodom Had No Bible* (Minneapolis: Bethany House, n.d.) n.p.n. Used by permission.

3. Stephen F. Olford, *Heart-Cry for Revival* (Memphis, TN: Encounter Ministries, Inc., n.d.) n.p.n. Used by permission.

4. Darrell Robinson, *Total Church Life* (Nashville: Broadman Press, 1985) n.p.n Used by permission.

5. Bill Hogue, *Love Leaves No Choice* (Dallas, Texas: Word, Inc., n.d.) n.p.n. Used by permission.

6. Elton Trueblood, *The Company of the Committed* (New York: Harper and Row Publishers, Inc., n.d.) n.p.n. Used by permission.

7. Stephen F. Olford, *Heart-Cry for Revival,* n.p.n.